D0619415

Life After Ramen

A cooking and entertaining guide for twentysomethings

By Ann Thatcher and Randy MacDonald

With gratitude to our husbands
for their love and support and to
our children for their inspiration

Introduction

You've mastered Ramen and you've eaten more than your fair share of fast food. You're older and wiser, your tastes more refined. You're ready for *Life After Ramen*.

Life After Ramen is full of delicious recipes with a gourmet bent. We've modified even the most difficult recipes so that they are impressive yet easy to follow. Realizing that you want to entertain on a more sophisticated level, we've not only included menus (ranging from a Fiesta to a Thanksgiving Dinner), we've also added suggestions for table decorations and wine pairings.

Our book emphasizes that the key to great eating and entertaining is careful planning and shopping. By following the tips available at the beginning of each chapter you will be able to create delicious, nutritious, and economical meals at home.

Enjoy your friends, enjoy cooking, but most of all enjoy your Life After Ramen!

Life After Ramen
A Cooking & Entertaining Guide For Twentysomethings

By Ann Thatcher and Randy MacDonald

Published by Reeny B. & Company

Layout and Design by E. Sawinski

Illustration Concepts by E. Sawinski and A. Truan, Knoxville, TN

Typesetting by Hannah Thatcher, Knoxville, TN

Copyright ©2010

ISBN 9780615249964

Library of Congress 2009906439

Printed in USA

This book is a compilation of recipes favored by the authors and may or may not be original recipes.

To obtain additional copies of Life After Ramen

VISIT:
www.lifeafterramencookbook.com

Contents

Taking Stock: Kitchen Basics

Having the right ingredients and the right tools on hand makes cooking so much easier. If you don't have all of these, consider adding a new item each week or request the larger items as gifts.

Stock Your Pantry

Baking Items
All-purpose flour
Salt
Granulated sugar
Baking soda
Baking powder
Vanilla

Oils
Canola oil
Olive oil
Spray oil
Sesame oil

Herbs and Spices
Dried basil
Cumin powder
Pepper
Crushed red pepper
Ground ginger
Seasoned salt
Oregano
Ground cinnamon
Salt and pepper

Sauces
Soy sauce
Apple cider vinegar
Worcestershire sauce
Hot sauce
Rice vinegar

Kitchen Utensils

10" chef's knife or cleaver

Rubber spatula

4-6" paring knife

Metal spatula

Grater

Wooden spoons

Electric hand mixer

Tongs

Cutting board

Can opener

Colander

Measuring cups and spoons

Large stainless steel serving spoon

Large stainless steel slotted spoon

Pot and Pan Basics

**Stainless steel cookware
is preferred; not non-stick:**

10-12" skillet with lid*

8 quart stock pot with lid*

2 and 5 quart pots with lids*

11" x 17" baking sheets

Glass mixing bowls

2-9" round cake pans

9" x 13" glass casserole dish

9" x 13" metal roasting pan

*Inexpensive sets are readily available and often
on sale. Restaurant supply stores offer commercial
grade cookware at reasonable prices.*

Refrigerator Basics

Milk

Eggs

Butter

Parmesan Cheese

Freezer Basics

Bags of frozen green vegetables
(broccoli, green beans, etc.)

Loaf of bread

Ready-made pie crust

China Cabinet

4-8 place settings of matching dishes,

stainless flatware, water glasses, and

wine glasses *(Can be purchased at discount
stores inexpensively. Buy plain white or cream
dishes for versatility.)*

Linens

4 dishtowels

Sponges

Table napkins
*(Can be purchased inexpensively
for special occasions)*

Oven mitt

Pot holders

How to Buy: **Produce**

Choosing fruits and vegetables from the large variety offered at the grocery store can sometimes be confusing. Generally, fruits and vegetables taste best and are more economical in their peak season. The following guidelines, based on information from the USDA, will assist you in selecting the best produce possible. As new varieties are constantly being introduced, it is wise to get to know your produce department clerk who is usually happy to help.

Fruit	Season	Store	Guidelines
Apples	Sept.-May	Refrig.	Look for firm fruit that is rich in color with no blemishes. Educate yourself on tart vs. sweet varieties.
Avocadoes	All year	Ripen at room temp. then refrig.	This fruit varies in color from green to black, and in size from small to large. Ripened when yields to thumb pressure. Avoid mushiness.
Bananas	All year	Room Temp.	Look for firm and bright yellow. Avoid bruises.
Blueberries	June-Sept.	Refrig.	Look for plump and uniform in size. Avoid shriveled berries and check for mold.
Citrus fruits	Oct.-June	Refrig.	Look for firm fruit that is heavy for its size. Thin skinned fruit tends to be juicier. Avoid coarse skin.
Grapes	June-Dec.	Refrig.	Look for plump, well-formed fruit, firmly attached to stem. Avoid wrinkled or brown stems.
Melons (cantaloupe)	May- Sept.	Ripen at room temp. Chill before serving.	Look for yellow skin and a sweet smell. Ripened when stem end yields slightly to pressure. Avoid green skin.

Fruit (continued)	Season	Store	Guidelines
Melons (Honey-Dew)	July-Oct.	Ripen at room temp. Chill before serving.	Look for pale yellow-green skin and a sweet smell. Avoid if skin is white and hard.
Melons (Watermelon)	May-Aug.	Refrig. cut melon	Easier to judge cut melon: Look for good red color and dark seeds. Avoid white streaks and white seeds.
Peaches / Nectarines	June-Sept.	Room Temp.	Look for plump and rich in color. Avoid hard or green.
Pears	Aug.-May	Room Temp.	Look for firm and rich color- many varieties: ask clerks in produce dept.
Strawberries	June-Aug.	Refrig.	Look for firm, plump, full red color; attached stems. Avoid shrunken or moldy (look at bottom of container for mold)

• •

Vegetables	Season	Store	Guidelines
Asparagus	March- June	Refrig.	Look for tight tips; firm stalks. Avoid open tips.
Beans (Snap)	All year	Refrig.	Look for bright green & firm. Avoid limp with brown spots.
Broccoli	Oct.-May	Refrig.	Look for compact dark green buds. Avoid open, yellow buds
Corn	May-Sept.	Refrig.	Look for fresh green husks. Avoid wilted, dry husks and silks.
Lettuce (green leaf or romaine)	All year	Crisper drawer of Refrig.	Look for bright colors. Avoid brown edges.
Lettuce (Iceberg)	All year	Crisper drawer of Refrig.	Look for rounded, medium weight. Avoid brown spots
Mushrooms (button)	All year	Remove from plastic Cover w/ paper towel. Refrig.	Look for white, caps tight around stem. Avoid dark color gills.
Squash (zucchini)	June-Aug.	Refrig.	Look for firm, bright green color; med size. Avoid dull, blemishes
Tomatoes (really a fruit)	May-Aug.	Refrig. after ripened	Look for firm, rich color. Avoid soft; blemishes.

How to Buy: Meat, Poultry, and Seafood

If you are not a vegetarian, chances are meat, poultry, and seafood are a main part of your diet. Not only are they a high source of protein, but they also contain B vitamins, iron, zinc, and essential fatty acids. Basic tips for purchasing include:

- Consider the amount of TIME you have to cook and select your meat, poultry, or seafood accordingly. A pot roast will take longer to cook than a piece of fresh fish.

- NEVER buy past the expiration date!

- ALWAYS keep refrigerated items cold to avoid bacterial contamination.

- SMELLS that are strong are usually a sign that the product is starting to deteriorate.

Buying Meat (Beef and Pork)

Select by grade: USDA Choice or USDA Select is leaner than USDA Prime which is the highest quality and the most flavorful. However, USDA Prime usually has the highest fat content. Less tender cuts usually take longer to cook and include the following:

Round Roast*	Chuck Roast*
Brisket*	Flank Steak
London Broil	Sirloin Tip Roast
Pork Chops	Pork Ribs*

Requires more cooking time.

More tender cuts which may be cooked quickly include the following:

Filet Mignon	Sirloin
Porterhouse Steak	Prime Rib
Standing Rib Roast	Beef/Pork Tenderloins
Rib-eye Steak	

Color: Choose beef that is bright red and pork that is pink in color for optimum freshness. Avoid meats that are brown or have a green cast.

Fat Percent Labels: Most grocers offer labeled ground beef/pork with percentages of fat by weight. It's healthy to choose the lowest percentage of weight.

Cuts that have little fat are best when marinated and cooked quickly:

London Broil   Flank Steak

Sirloin Tip

Cuts that need to be covered and cooked in liquid:

Round Roast   Chuck

Sirloin Tip   Brisket

Buying Poultry (Chicken and Turkey)

Select by grade: Buy U.S. Grade A only.

Color: Poultry should be pale pink in color to ensure freshness. Any sign of discoloration may be sign of deterioration.

Texture: Poultry should be firm to the touch.

Buying Seafood

Source: Purchase seafood from a reliable source, buying seafood from the "back of a truck" may seem economical, but this is a risky endeavor.

Appearance: Fresh fish has a moist and bright surface and is firm to the touch.

Smell: Fresh seafood will not have a strong "fishy" smell.

Menus for a Month

Time is limited: make it easy and make it fast!

Follow this planning and shopping guide and you'll be
sitting down to at least three wholesome meals each week in
less time than it takes to go out. These easy and fast meals will
be healthier for you and your budget.

Think:

Entrée the main recipe which requires the most time to prepare (maybe a weekend meal?). *

Encore quick and easy dishes made from entrée leftovers.*

Food in a Flash super quick meals put together with pantry or freezer items, or restaurant pick-ups.

All Entrée and Encore recipes may be found in the index.

Week 1

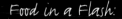

Entrée: *

Marinated Flank Steak

Consommé Rice

Broccoli Florets

Encore: *

Flank Steak Sandwiches

Corn on the Cob with Basil Butter

Food in a Flash:

Three Cheese Tortellini with Spaghetti Sauce

Salad

Shopping List:
1-2 lbs flank steak
1 can beef consommé soup
English muffins
Swiss cheese
Three cheese tortellini *(found in dairy section)*
Jar of spaghetti sauce
Lettuce
Bagged salad
Broccoli
Corn on the cob
Instant rice
Red wine

Pantry items:
Soy sauce
Olive oil
Garlic
Parmesan cheese
Butter
Basil
Dijon mustard
Onion

*All Entrée and Encore recipes may be found in the index.

Week 2

Entrée: *

Pan Roasted Salmon

Spinach with Pine Nuts and Apples

Microwaved Baked Potatoes

Encore: *

Salmon Salad with Lemon Dressing

Parmesan Toast Strips

Food in a Flash:

Company Tomato Soup

Gourmet Grilled Cheese
(use either Pepper Jack, Swiss, Smoked Cheddar, or a combination of cheeses)

Shopping List:
1½ lbs fresh salmon
Two 1lb bags spinach
1 cup pine nuts
1 Granny Smith apple
2 Russet potatoes
1 bunch green onions
1 head Romaine lettuce
Grape tomatoes
2 lemons
Loaf of bread *(freeze leftover bread)*
Corn flakes
¼ cup sun-dried tomatoes
Specialty cheese

Pantry items:
Lemon pepper
Olive oil
Parmesan cheese
Garlic
Butter
Salt
Dill or Basil
One 10¾ oz can
   tomato soup
One 14 oz can petite
   diced tomatoes
Pepper

All Entrée and Encore recipes may be found in the index.

Week 3

Entrée:*

Spaghetti with Meatballs

Basic Bowl of Greens

Garlic Bread**

Encore:*

Meatball Sandwiches

Twenty-Two Second Coleslaw

Food in a Flash:

Chicken Strips *(from your favorite drive-thru)*

Twenty-Two Second Coleslaw

Shopping List:

1 lb Italian sausage
28 oz can tomatoes
15 oz can tomato sauce
6 oz can tomato paste
7 oz pkg of pasta *(spaghetti or linguine)*
Poppy seeds
1½ lbs ground chuck
Lettuce
Sub rolls
Mozzarella cheese
One 16 oz pkg prepared coleslaw mix
One 10 oz pkg frozen baby peas

Pantry List:

Egg
Onion
Parsley
Salt
Pepper
Crushed red pepper
Basil
Bread crumbs
Sugar
Olive oil
Canola oil
White vinegar
Pecans

**To make garlic bread: Cut sub rolls in half; spread with butter and sprinkle with garlic salt and Parmesan cheese. Broil.

*All Entrée and Encore recipes may be found in the index.

Chicken Stir-Fry

Rice

White Chicken Chili with Tomatoes

Cheesy Cornbread Muffins

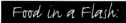

Barbequed ribs *(from your favorite drive-thru)*

Garlic Roasted Green Beans

Cheesy Cornbread Muffins *(leftover)*

Shopping List:
1 large deli roasted chicken
1½ cup snow peas
½ cup cashew pieces
One 28 oz can petite diced tomatoes
One 13 oz container fresh salsa *(in produce dept.)*
1 lime
1 bunch cilantro
2 cups Monterrey Jack cheese
Three 15 oz cans Great Northern beans
2 cups self-rising corn meal
1 cup extra sharp cheddar cheese
½ cup sour cream
½ cup buttermilk**
1 cup cottage cheese
1 lb can Allen's™ Italian green beans
10 oz can garlic-flavored chicken broth

Pantry List:
Soy sauce
Salt
Cumin
Sugar
Sesame oil
Two 10 oz cans chicken broth
2 small onions
Butter
3 eggs
Rice

**Buttermilk substitute: add 1 tbsp vinegar to 1 cup milk.

All Entrée and Encore recipes may be found in the index.

Special Occasion Planner

Entertaining is a snap with our menus and decorating ideas.

Dazzle your friends with a Martini Party, your family with

a Traditional Thanksgiving Feast, or that special

someone with a Romantic Dinner for Two.

Our menus are easy to prepare and the results – terrific!

All these menus can be used for a variety of occasions:

simply change the decorations to fit your party themes.

You'll find all these recipes in the index

unless otherwise noted.

• •

Good Host/Good Guest Guidelines

Whether you've invited the boss for dinner or friends for drinks, the essential guidelines for successful entertaining remain constant.

The Good Host:

- Cleans the areas where guests gather.
- Has a clean bathroom, with plenty of toliet paper and a clean hand towel.
- Has enough plates, flatware, glasses, and napkins.
- Prepares as much food in advance as possible.
- Uses flowers, candles, and music to help set the mood.

The Good Guest:

- Responds promptly and definitively to an invitation.
- Brings a small hostess gift *(flowers, cocktail napkins, wine, candy...)*
- Puts napkin in lap when seated at the table.
- Keeps elbow off the table.
- Keeps mouth closed when chewing.
- Begins eating after the hostess takes the first bite.
- Places used silverware on the plate.
- Keeps cell phone off.
- Helps clean up after dinner.
- Thanks the hostess.

Table settings

A nicely set table makes your guests feel special.

Follow this diagram for a sit-down dinner:

Dinner Table Setting

1. Bread and butter plate
2. Water glass
3. Optional drinking glass
4. Napkin
5. Salad fork
6. Dinner fork
7. Dessert fork or spoon
8. Soup bowl and salad plate
9. Dinner plate
10. Dinner knife
11. Teaspoon
12. Soup spoon

Tips:

- Use utensils from the outside in.

- Put index finger and thumb together on both hands Left hand forms a "b" for bread and the right hand forms a "d" for drinks. Use this as a reminder that the bread plate goes to the left and the drinks go to the right of the dinner plate.

- Cutting edge of knife faces the dinner plate.

Buffet Table Setting

Tips:

- Have separate tables for food and drinks.

- If guests are eating on their laps, try to serve food that only requires a fork.

- Wrap silverware in a napkin for ease in carrying.

- Desserts work well on a dinner buffet if there is space. It may be more efficient to have a separate dessert table.

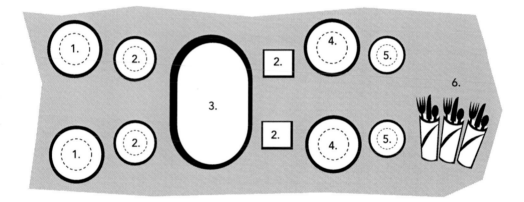

Remember:

1. plates
2. sides/ veggies
3. entree
4. salad
5. bread
6. napkins/ silverware

Party Countdown

A little advanced planning and preparation will keep you out of the kitchen and in the middle of all the fun.

Two weeks before decide on the following:

- Type of party *(large/small, formal/casual, dinner/cocktails, dessert, etc.)*.

- Date, Time *(check the calendar and several of the "key" guests to avoid scheduling conflicts)*.

- The menu. Will you cook everything or ask others to contribute?

- Send invitations. The invitation sets the "tone" for the party. If the party is casual, send a fun card; if dressier, send a more formal invitation. A really good invitation will answer all the questions the guest might have. Besides stating who the host is, the address, and the time, include whether or not a meal will be served, and what the guests are expected to wear.

Six days before:

- Purchase non-perishables such as paper products (napkins, cups, plates, and toilet paper), alcoholic and non-alcoholic beverages.

Three days before:

- Clean the areas where your guests will gather.

- Decide on music and have CD's ready.

Two days before:

- Check your recipes and make a list of all necessary ingredients.

- Do the bulk of your shopping today including meat, fresh produce, and flowers.

- Decide on which dishes, flatware, glassware, and serving pieces you will use and set aside *(we like making a list of which food item will be served on which platter, bowl, etc.)*.

One day before:

- Set the table and make flower arrangements.

- Cook as much in advance as possible. Many desserts, casseroles, marinades, salad dressings, and entrees can be assembled or made a day ahead.

- Decide what you will be wearing and have it cleaned and ready to go.

- Set up the bar area.

Party Day!

- Buy ice, if needed, and place in cooler.

- Touch up the house *(empty trash, freshen bathroom, empty dishwasher)*.

- Set a timetable for food preparation so you will know when an item needs to be baked, tossed, poured, etc.

- Relax and enjoy your guests!

Bar Tips:

- You don't want to spend your evening being the bartender so narrow the options of liquor to be served *(offer beer with a red or white wine or beer with one type of speciality drink)*. Consider asking a friend to help with bartending duties.

- Have a good stock of non-alcoholic beverages available including water.

- Have plenty of ice *(1 lb of ice per person is a good rule of thumb)*.

- Depending on your choice of drinks, be sure to have the following handy:
    Bottle openers- beer, wine, and soft drinks
    Ice bucket and scoop
    Blender, if mixing
    Cocktail napkins
    Lemon/lime slices
    Mixers

New Year's Eve Buffet

Gingered Pork Tenderloin on Yeast Rolls

Chicken Strips *(precooked)*

Artichoke Jalapeno Dip w/ Garlic Pita Chips

Fruit Stuffed Pineapple w/ Lemon Cream Dip

Cream Puffs *(in the frozen dessert section)*

Brownies *(from bakery)*

Champagne or Prosecco

Decorations:

- Place a vase of 'cash and carry' red roses in a black paper top hat. Fill obvious spaces with greenery cut from a yard *(yew and magnolia work well as fillers).*

- Sprinkle silver confetti on the table; add some unrolled confetti streamers, horns and other noisemakers.

- Put white votive candles in clear holders on either side of the hat.

- Float silver, black, and red balloons on the ceiling.

Dinner for Two

Antipasto platter*

Quick focaccia

Basic bowl of greens

Shrimp scampi over linguine

Strawberries dipped in chocolate

Pinot Grigio

Use small amounts of specialty cheeses, salamis, olives, and crackers on a larger platter.

Decorations:

- Use a white tablecloth and napkins.
- Light lots of white candles in clear votives.
- Arrange 'cash and carry' flowers in small vases or create one large centerpiece.
- Low lights and soft music make for a romantic evening!

Spring Brunch

Smoked Salmon Platter

Seasonal Fresh Fruit with Honey/ Lemon Dressing

Old Standby Sausage-Egg Casserole

Assorted Sweet Rolls or Coffee Cake *(bakery purchase)*

Bloody Mary's*

*Bloody Mary's- Buy Bloody Mary mixes at your local grocery.
May be served with or without alcohol. Garnish with a stalk of celery.

Decorations:

- Purchase multi-colored violas *(Johnny Jump-ups)* from a garden store or nursery. Put violas in small baskets or clay pots, tucking moss around outside edges. Place in the center of the table covered with white or yellow cloth.

- Use pale purple and/or yellow napkins.

Other options:

- Use glass vases filled with pastel colored jelly beans, dyed Easter eggs on a platter with Easter grass *(or shredded paper which is neater)*.

- Use tiny baskets with Easter grass and a few jelly beans at each place setting.

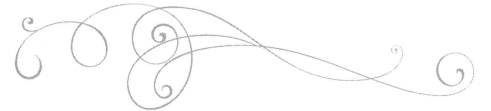

Bridal Shower

Cheese Straws (*purchased*)

Mandarin Orange Salad

Tomato Basil Tart

Angel Food Sherbet Cake

Mimosas*

*Mimosas: Fill a champagne glass half-full with orange juice.
Top with champagne. Garnish with a strawberry. Cheers!

Decorations:

- Use the bride's colors for flowers and napkins. 'Cash and carry' flowers may be purchased relatively inexpensively at grocery stores and floral shops to create a centerpiece (*or consider small vases of flowers at each place setting*).

- Purchase an inexpensive costume veil from a party store for the bride to wear.

- Obtain old photos of the bride and groom from their families to display in the entry or dining table.

- Make a 'rehearsal' bouquet: after opening a gift, push the ends of the ribbons through a hole punched in the center of a paper plate, leaving the loops on the top of the plate. After all the gifts are open, the result is a colorful ribbon bouquet that the bride may carry at the wedding rehearsal.

Traditional Thanksgiving Feast

Roasted Turkey

Holiday Dressing

Cranberry Relish

Broccoli Florets

Mashed Potatoes/Gravy

Yeast Rolls *(purchased)*

Pumpkin Pie

Pecan Pie

Chardonnay

Decorations:

- Use all the wonderful fall colors *(gold, green, orange, and red)* in candles and napkins.

- A hollowed-out medium sized pumpkin filled with mums or small pumpkins scattered on the table with votives are alternatives to a cornucopia.

Old Fashioned Sunday Dinner
Like Dinner at Grandma's

Nana's Pot Roast with Carrots

Green Beans

Mashed Potatoes

Rolls *(purchased)*

Lemon Ice Box Pie

Sweetened Iced Tea

Decorations:

- Use checked tablecloths and napkins or purchase retro tablecloths at antique malls or flea markets.

- Place daisies *(purchased from the grocery store or 'cash and carry' florist)* in an old pitcher or in Ball jars on the table.

Fiesta

Chicken Fajitas

Guacamole with Tortilla Chips

Black Bean Salsa

Mango Ginger Ice Cream

Margaritas*

*Margarita mix can be purchsed in a bucket for freezing or pre-made at the liquor store.

Decorations:

- The brighter the better! Use Mexican blankets or colorful tablecloths in yellow, turqouise, red, and orange.

- Scatter bright tissue paper flowers or clay pots of sunflowers on the table.

- Set the mood with a salsa CD. Ole!

Martini Party

Layered Shrimp Dip w/ Tortilla chips

Stuffed Mushrooms

Brie w/ Assorted fruits

Bowl of nuts

Flavored martinis

Decorations:

- Purchase inexpensive martini glasses and a cocktail shaker

  at a pottery outlet or discount store.

- Buy fun cocktail napkins.

**Note: Martinis are best served ice cold! Put glasses, shaker,
and vodka in freezer until ready to use.**

Lemon Drop Martini

3 shots citrus flavored vodka

3 shots orange flavored liqueur

1 cup ice cubes

2 shots fresh lemon juice

Sugar

Lemon slices for garnish

Swipe lemon around rim of chilled martini glasses; dip rim into saucer of sugar.
Shake vodka, orange flavored liqueur, and lemon juice in a shaker with ice
cubes. Strain into prepared glasses.

Serves 2

Chocolate Martini

3 shots vodka

3 shots chocolate liqueur

5 shots half 'n half

3 shots crème de cacao

Cocoa powder

Cherries

When ready to serve, dip glass into saucer of cocoa powder. Shake liquid
ingredients with a cup of ice. Strain and pour into glasses. Top with a cherry garnish.

Serves 2

Classic Martini

3 shots gin

4 drops dry vermouth

2 or more olives

Pour gin into shaker with ice. Shake and let sit while
placing 2 drops of vermouth into each of two glasses.
Strain and pour into glasses. Add olives to garnish.

Serves 2

Cosmopolitan

4 shots citrus flavored vodka

2 shots fresh lime juice

2 shots triple sec

1 shot cranberry juice

Lime slices

Combine all ingredients in shaker with ice. Shake, strain,
and pour into glasses. Garnish with lime slice.

Serves 2

Pack a Picnic

Pork Tenderloin in Citrus Juices

Rolls *(bakery purchase)*

Edamame

Tabouleh Salad

Raclette cheese

Seedless red grapes

Pinot Noir

Decorations:

- Invest in a picnic basket to set a festive tone.
- Pack a quilt or checked tablecloth with coordinating napkins.
- Dress up paper plates with wicker holders.
- For an evening picnic, pack votive candles.
- Don't forget the corkscrew!

Appetizers

Appetizers

Appetizers set the mood for your party – whether it's a dinner party, a cocktail party, or friends stopping by unexpectedly. Our tips for appetizers will make your next party enjoyable not only for your guests, but also for you.

Tips:

- Consider what else is being served: heavy meal, light appetizers *(set out a bowl of smoked almonds or shelled edamame)*; soup and salad dinner, served something more substantial such as Spinach-Artichoke Dip and bagel crisps.

- Match the appetizer to the entrée or theme *(i.e. if the entrée is fajitas, have Pineapple Salsa and tortilla chips for the appetizer.)*

- Keep an assortment of "Food in a Flash" items *(listed on the following page)* in your pantry and freezer for unexpected company.

Stayed late at work and company's coming? Assemble these quick and

delicious appetizers in a Flash! These appetizers look great arranged on

a large plate or platter:

Antipasto Platter (all these items are available in the deli section of the grocery):
Hot Pepper Jack cheese, sliced or cubed
Sharp Cheddar cheese, sliced or cubed
Thinly sliced specialty salamis (peppered, Genoa, or Summer Sausage)
Assorted crackers
Gourmet olives
Grape tomatoes

Hot Wing Hoopla:
Hot wings, purchased
Celery sticks
Carrot sticks
Blue cheese or Ranch dip (purchase in the produce section)

Specialty Cheeses and Crackers:
1 wedge Saga Blue cheese
1 round of Brie
Assorted crackers
A bunch of seedless green or red grapes, washed and chilled.
Or
Boursin cheese
Water crackers
Pear or apple slices (dipped in orange or lemon juice to prevent browning)
Or
Port Wine cheese ball with pecans
Assorted crackers

More Appetizers in a Flash!

Keep these items in the pantry and fridge for drop in company or snacks:

Salted almonds

Edamame *(buy frozen, thaw, drain, and salt to taste)*

Hummus and pita chips

Gourmet salsa *(in deli or produce section)* and blue tortilla chips

Guacamole *(in deli section)* and tortilla chips

Shrimp rings with cocktail sauce *(buy frozen)*

Olives

Grape tomatoes

Japanese rice crackers

Wasabi green peas

Mixed nuts

Cheese straws

Crab Bites

Can be an appetizer or a good dinner with a bowl of soup

One 7½ oz can lump crab meat*, drained

¼ cup mayonnaise

1 green onion, sliced

4 oz Swiss cheese, shredded

One 5 oz can water chestnuts, drained and chopped

1 tsp fresh lemon juice

½ tsp curry

1 roll flaky biscuits

- Preheat oven to 400°F.
- In a small bowl, mix together crab meat, mayonnaise, onion, cheese, lemon juice, curry and water chestnuts.
- Separate each biscuit into thirds and place on baking sheet.
- Top each biscuit with a dollop of crab mixture.
- Bake for 10-12 minutes.

Serves 4-6

* Crab can contain small pieces of shell & cartilage. Gently pick through crab to remove.

Wasabi-Salmon Spread

1 cup roasted salmon, crumbled

One 8 oz pkg cream cheese, softened

¼ - ½ cup milk

¼ cup red onion, finely chopped

¼ tsp dill weed

1½ tsp wasabi *(found in the Asian food aisle)* *

salt and pepper to taste

1-2 cucumbers sliced into ¼ inch slices, patted dry

Assorted crackers

- Mix the first 7 ingredients together.
- Serve on slices of cucumber and/or crackers.

Serves a crowd

* Wasabi is very hot. Depending on your taste, more or less may be used.

Smoked Salmon Platter
Impress your brunch or cocktail party guests

1 lb pkg smoked salmon

One 8 oz pkg cream cheese, softened

One 4 oz jar capers, drained

½ medium red onion, diced

4 hard boiled eggs, chopped

One 10 oz pkg mini-bagels, sliced in half

- Place the salmon in the center of a large platter surrounded by mounds of the remaining ingredients.
- Serve with small spreaders.

Serves 8-10

Oyster/Shrimp Shooters

12 small, fresh, raw oysters or 12 medium shrimp, cooked and peeled

Cocktail sauce

12 shot glasses *(inexpensive ones may be found at pottery or glass outlets)*

- Place 2 teaspoons of cocktail sauce in the bottom of each shot glass.
- Top with an oyster or shrimp and shoot!

Serves 6 (2 shooters each)

Shrimp Spread

One 3 oz pkg cream cheese, softened

1 tsp green onion, chopped
(save some of the dark green stem rings for garnish)

¼ cup mayonnaise

Dash of Tabasco™ sauce

One 4¼ oz can baby shrimp, drained

1 tsp of lemon juice

Butter crackers

- Mix cream cheese, chopped green onion, mayonnaise, Tabasco™, and lemon juice together in a medium bowl.
- Fold in shrimp.
- Place in a small serving bowl and sprinkle with a few dark green onion rings.
- Serve with butter crackers

Serves 4

Pepper/ Feta Bites

1 red bell pepper, cut into 1" squares

8 oz carton feta cheese

- Preheat broiler.
- Place pepper squares on baking sheet and fill with feta cheese.
  (You could cover with plastic wrap and refrigerate a day in advance.)
- Broil until lightly browned.
- Place on a plate and serve hot.

Serves 4

Mexican Roll-Ups

4 large flour tortillas

Two 8 oz pkgs cream cheese, softened

1 oz envelope ranch dressing mix

One 4 oz can green chilies

One 4 oz can ripe olives, chopped

One 4 oz jar pimentos, chopped

2 green onions, sliced

2 cups salsa

- Drain green chilies, olives, and pimentos on paper towels until liquid is absorbed.
- In a medium bowl, mix cream cheese and ranch dressing.
- Stir in green chilies, olives, pimentos, and green onions.
- Spread one fourth of the cream cheese mixture onto each tortilla then roll them up.
- Wrap in plastic wrap and refrigerate for at least 2 hours.
- When ready to serve, slice into 1 inch slices and place on a serving plate with a bowl of salsa for dipping in the center.

Serves 6-8

Guacamole

2 avocados, washed

½ lemon, juiced *(keeps avocado from turning brown)*

½ medium onion, chopped fine

½ tsp salt

1 tbsp olive oil

1-2 dashes Tabasco™ sauce, more if desired

Tortilla chips

- Cut the avocados in half and removed the seed.
- Scoop into a small bowl and mash with a fork.
- Mix in the lemon juice, onion, salt, olive oil, and Tabasco™.
- Cover and refrigerate for 1 hour.
- Serve with chips.

Serves a crowd

Tex Mex Layered Dip

Two 9 oz cans bean dip *(found in the chip aisle)*

8 oz sour cream

½ cup mayonnaise

One 1.25 oz envelope taco seasoning mix

¼ cup red onion, diced

2 tomatoes, seeded and chopped

One 15 oz can sliced ripe olives *(optional)*

1 small avocado, chopped *(optional)*

1½ cups sharp cheddar cheese, grated

Tortilla chips

- Spread both cans of bean dip into a glass pie plate or casserole dish.
- Mix sour cream, mayonnaise, and taco seasoning together in a small bowl.
- Spoon a layer of the sour cream/taco seasoning mixture over the bean dip.
- Layer the remaining ingredients starting with the onion and finishing with the cheese.
- Cover with plastic wrap and refrigerate for at least an hour.
- Serve with tortilla chips.

Serves a crowd

Layered Shrimp Dip

Bottom Layer

Two 8 oz pkgs cream cheese, softened

2 tbsp mayonnaise

1 tbsp lemon juice

1 tsp lemon pepper

½ tsp seasoned salt

Top Layer

One 12 oz bottle cocktail sauce

1lb shrimp, cooked, peeled, deveined, and chopped

1½ cups Monterrey Jack cheese, shredded

3 green onions, chopped

1 medium tomato, chopped and seeded

Tortilla Chips

- Cream bottom layer ingredients with a mixer.
- Spread in a 9"x13" glass baking dish or on a 12" round platter.
- Pour cocktail sauce over cream cheese mixture.
- When ready to serve, top with layers of remaining ingredients.
- Serve with tortilla chips.

Serves a crowd

Spinach Artichoke Dip

2 tbsp olive oil

1 onion, diced

Two 10 oz pkgs chopped frozen spinach, thawed and squeezed dry

Two 8 oz pkgs cream cheese, softened

Two 8.5 oz cans artichoke hearts, drained and chopped

1 cup mayonnaise

1 cup sour cream

Hot sauce to taste

Salt and pepper to taste

½-1 cup Parmesan cheese

Spray oil

Garlic bagel chips

- Preheat oven to 350°F.
- Using a medium to high heat, sauté the onions in oil until tender. Add the spinach and cook until all moisture is removed.
- In a medium size bowl, add the onions and spinach to the cream cheese and stir until well blended.
- Add the artichokes, mayonnaise, sour cream, hot sauce, and Parmesan cheese. Salt and pepper to taste. Mix well.
- Pour into a lightly greased casserole dish.
- Bake for 30-45 minutes until hot and bubbly.
- Serve with garlic bagel chips.

Serves a crowd

Just Like Pizza Dip
"Watching the ballgame" fare

Spray oil

One 8 oz pkg cream cheese, softened

One 14 oz jar pizza sauce

3 green onions, sliced

½ cup green pepper, chopped

One 6 oz can black olives, sliced and drained

2 cups Mozzarella cheese, shredded

3 oz sliced pepperoni, chopped

Corn chips

- Preheat oven to 350°F.
- Lightly spray glass pie plate with oil.
- With a spoon, spread cream cheese into bottom of plate.
- Cover cream cheese with layer of pizza sauce. Continue to layer with remaining ingredients.
- Bake for 20 minutes.
- Serve with chips.

Serves 6-8

Baked Artichoke/Jalapeno Dip

Spray oil

1¾ cup mayonnaise

Two 14 oz. cans artichoke hearts, drained and chopped

1½ cups shredded Mozzarella cheese, divided

½ cup grated Parmesan cheese, divided

One 4 oz can chopped jalapenos, drained

Garlic bagel chips

- Preheat the oven to 350°F.
- Lightly spray a 2 quart casserole dish with oil.
- Mix the mayonnaise, artichoke hearts, 1 cup of Mozzarella cheese, ¼ cup of Parmesan cheese, and the jalapenos together in a medium bowl.
- Spoon into the casserole dish and top with remaining Parmesan and Mozzarella.
- Bake for 25 minutes or until the top is lightly browned and the casserole is bubbly.
- Serve with garlic bagel chips.

Serves 8-10

Garlic Cheese Dip

8 oz pkg cream cheese, softened

One 5 oz jar Kraft Old English Cheese™ *(found in the dairy section of the store)*

1 tsp garlic salt

Crudites of choice: celery and carrot sticks, green and red bell pepper strips, grape tomatoes, raw cauliflower, etc.

- Blend cheeses and garlic salt with a mixer. Spoon into a serving bowl. Cover with plastic wrap.
- Refrigerate overnight allowing flavors to blend.
- When ready to serve, place in the center of a large plate or platter surrounded by raw vegetables.

Serves a crowd

Bruschetta with Pesto

1 baguette French bread, sliced into ½" rounds

One 7 oz container prepared pesto

4 Roma tomatoes, thinly sliced
(may substitute chopped red and yellow grape tomatoes)

Fresh Parmesan or Mozzarella cheese, shredded

- Preheat the oven to broil.
- Place slices of bread under broiler until just lightly toasted.
- Spread each slice of bread with pesto; top with tomato and cheese.
- Broil again until cheese melts.
- Serve immediately.

Serves 8-10

Stuffed Mushrooms

6 slices of bacon

32 large button mushrooms, wiped clean with a damp paper towel

8 tbsp onion, finely chopped

4 tbsp butter

8 tbsp bread crumbs

2 tbsp parsley, chopped

2 tsp salt

Pepper to taste

¼ tsp basil

- Preheat oven to 375°F.
- Fry the bacon and crumble.
- Pour off all but 2 tablespoons of the bacon grease from the pan.
- Remove mushroom stems and chop stems into small pieces.
- In the same pan as the bacon grease, melt the butter over medium heat.
- Sauté the onions and chopped mushroom stems until soft.
- Remove from heat and stir in the remaining ingredients.
- With a spoon, press a small mound of filling into each mushroom cap and place on a baking sheet.
- Bake for 10 minutes.
- Use tongs to place on a small serving dish garnished with parsley.
- Serve hot.

Serves 8

Pineapple Salsa

Impressive topping for grilled pork, fish and chicken

2 cups fresh pineapple, cut into ¼ inch cubes *(may substitute mango for pineapple)*

½ cup red bell pepper, diced

½ cup green bell pepper, diced

3 cloves garlic, minced

½ *(well-packed)* cup fresh cilantro, chopped

½ -1 jalapeno pepper, seeded and minced

½ lime, juiced

1 tsp brown sugar

½ tsp salt

½ tsp ground cumin

- Combine all ingredients in a medium bowl and mix well.

Serves 4

FYI: Wonderful as an appetizer served over softened cream cheese and served with tortilla chips.*Serves 6-8*

Mango Salsa

Good with chicken, fish or pork, or just as a dip with tortilla chips

1 large mango, peeled and cut into ¼" cubes

¼ cup red bell pepper, diced

1 jalapeno pepper, seeded and chopped *

1 tbsp fresh basil, chopped

1½ tsp red wine vinegar

2 tsp lime juice

½ tsp sugar

- Put mango and bell pepper in a large bowl. Set aside.
- Mix remaining ingredients together in a separate bowl.
- Pour over mango-pepper mixture and toss gently. Best if used the day it is made.

* Jalapeno peppers add heat to a dish, so add a small amount until desired heat is obtained. It is advisable to use latex or rubber gloves when chopping peppers as the heat will transfer to everything you touch. At the very least, wash your hands quickly after chopping.

Makes approximately 1½-2 cups

Black Bean Salsa

2 medium tomatoes, chopped

1 red bell pepper, chopped

One 12 oz can shoepeg corn, drained

¼ cup purple onion, finely chopped

Small chipotle pepper, chopped*

One 15 oz can black beans, rinsed and drained

⅓ cup fresh lime juice

¼ cup olive oil

⅓ cup cilantro, chopped

1 tsp salt

½ tsp ground cumin

¼ tsp ground pepper

Tortilla chips

- Put tomatoes, chopped red pepper, corn, onion, chipotle pepper, and beans in a large serving bowl.
- Combine lime juice, olive oil, cilantro, and spices in a small jar.
- Pour over vegetables and toss gently.
- Serve with tortilla chips.

Serves 6

*Note: Use caution when handling hot peppers. Be sure to wash hands thoroughly after handling as the heat will transfer to everything you touch.

The Very Versatile Cheese Quesadilla

2 large flour tortillas

1 cup shredded cheese of choice
(cheddar, Monterrey jack, pepper cheese...)

Spray oil

Salsa

Sour cream

- Heat a lightly oiled skillet over medium-high heat.
- Lay one tortilla in the bottom of the skillet; sprinkle the cheese evenly over the tortilla.
- Top with the remaining tortilla and cook 2 minutes on each side or until lightly browned. (You might use 2 spatulas for easier flipping).
- Remove the quesadilla from the pan and cut into wedges.
- Serve warm topped with a dollop of sour cream and salsa.

Serves 2-4

Filling variations:

Chopped green chili peppers

Chopped onion

Shrimp, cooked and chopped

Crab

Chicken, cooked and chopped

Make it a meal: Serve with tomato soup topped with fresh chopped cilantro!

Teriyaki Party Wings

Teriyaki Marinade

1 cup soy sauce

1 cup cooking sherry *(or water, white wine, or light rum)*

2 tbsp garlic powder

2 tbsp powdered ginger

½ cup sugar

16 chicken wings *(will yield 32 pieces)*

- Mix the marinade ingredients in a jar and set aside.
- Cut the wings in half at the joint and discard the meatless wing tip.
- Place the wings in a zippered plastic bag with the marinade and refrigerate overnight.
- Broil for 10 minutes, turn and broil 10 more minutes, or until skin is crispy on both sides.

Serves 8

Easy Homemade Hummus

2 cloves garlic, minced

Two15 oz cans garbanzo beans *(chick peas)*, drained

½ cup lemon juice

⅓ cup olive oil

1 tbsp sesame oil

Salt and Pepper to taste

Pita wedges

- Process or blend all ingredients together except pita wedges to a smooth consistency.
- Serve with pita wedges.

Serves 4-6

Cheese Ball

2 cups extra sharp cheddar cheese, shredded

One 8 oz pkg of cream cheese, softened

½ cup diced green pepper

½ tsp seasoned salt

1 tsp grated onion

Dash of Worcestershire sauce

Dash of hot sauce

Assorted crackers

- Combine the cheddar cheese and cream cheese together using a mixer or food processor.
- Add the remaining ingredients and mix well.
- Form into a ball.
- Cover with plastic wrap and refrigerate until ready to serve.
- Serve with a variety of crackers.

Serves a crowd

Soups & Salads

Soups and Salads

Soul satisfying soups and salads are delectable paired or delicious as individual entrées. Our soup recipes can feed a crowd and most of them may be frozen for future use. Our salads range from traditional to exotic and are always easy.

Tips for Soups:

- Check purchased soup labels for sodium content. Many tend to be high in this unhealthy additive. Buy low sodium varieties instead.

- Consider doubling recipes to freeze for future use. Cool and pour into gallon sized freezer bags.

- An 8-quart stock pot is useful to have on hand, not only for soups, but also for cooking pasta.

Tips for Salads:

- Buy greens that are crisp with no brown spots. Inspect bagged salad mixes for soggy pieces.

- All greens should be washed (including bagged mixes) and drained. (Consider buying a salad spinner- an inexpensive investment for quick, crispy salads.).

- Tear leaves just before assembling salads to prevent brown edges.

- Keep prepared greens in fridge until just before serving to ensure crispness.

Food in a Flash! Soups

Fresh and Frozen Soups: Many pre-made soups and gumbos are available in the freezer or deli section of the grocery. Embellish to make them seem homemade.

Embellishments

Cheese

Sour cream

Bacon bits

Chopped onion

Croutons

Cooked rice or noodles

Cooked meats

Fresh vegetables

Cooked beans

Food in a Flash! Salads

Bagged Salad Mixes: Using the greens as a base, use our recipes, or create wonderful one-of-a-kind salads using one or more of the Embellishments listed below.

Restaurant salads: Call ahead, pick up, and embellish!

Embellishments

Cooked sliced chicken or steak

Canned tuna *(or vacuum-packed)*

Artichoke hearts

Mandarin oranges

Sliced water chestnuts

Dried fruits such as cranberries or blueberries

Fresh fruits – apple, pears, strawberries

Fresh vegetables – onions, tomatoes, broccoli

Nuts – pecans, walnuts, almonds, pine nuts

Cheeses – feta, bleu, cheddar

Herbs and spices – basil, cilantro, oregano

Company Tomato Soup

¼ cup sun-dried tomatoes, packed in oil and diced

One 10¾ oz can tomato soup

1 soup can of water

One 14 oz can petite diced tomatoes

1 tsp dillweed or basil

Sour cream

- Put sun-dried tomatoes with oil in medium pot.
- Carefully stir the can of tomato soup into the hot oil; add water.
- Stir in tomatoes and dill or basil.
- Simmer 7-10 minutes.
- Add dollop of sour cream to each bowl.

Serves 4

Low Fat Turkey Chili

1 lb ground turkey

2 tbsp canola oil

½ cup onion, chopped

1 clove garlic, minced

1 tbsp cumin

¼ tsp crushed red pepper

2 tsp chili powder

One 28 oz can whole tomatoes, chopped

One 15 oz can stewed tomatoes

One 19 oz can chili beans, rinsed and drained

- Heat the canola oil in a large soup pot over medium-high heat. Add onion and garlic and cook just until onion is translucent.
- Add turkey; brown and crumble. Drain off fat.
- Add tomatoes and spices to pan. Bring to boil, then reduce heat and simmer for 15 minutes.
- Add beans and simmer for at least 30 minutes.

Serves 4-6

Easy Homestyle Chili

1 packet French's Chili-O™ seasoning mix

1 lb ground chuck

1 medium onion, chopped

2 tbsp canola oil

One 28 oz can petite diced tomatoes

1 cup water

1 can chili or kidney beans, drained

- Brown and crumble chuck in oil over medium heat; add onion and cook until tender. Drain off fat.
- Stir in the packet of seasoning mix.
- Add water, tomatoes, and beans and cook over medium heat for 10 minutes.
- Reduce heat and simmer for 30 minutes.

Serves 4-6

White Chicken Chili with Tomatoes

4 cooked chicken breasts or deli roasted chicken, shredded

One 28 oz can petite diced tomatoes

Three 15 oz cans Great Northern beans, rinsed and drained

1 small onion, chopped

One 14 oz container fresh salsa *(found in grocery deli)*

Two 10½ oz cans chicken broth

½ bunch cilantro, minced

1 tbsp cumin

1 tbsp lime juice

Monterrey Jack cheese, shredded

- In a soup pot, sauté onions in olive oil; add chicken broth.
- Stir in remaining ingredients and simmer for 30 minutes.
- Top each bowl with cheese.

Serves 4

Miso-Tofu Soup

Great source of protein

4 cups water

2 tbsp + miso paste*

½ cup firm tofu cut into ½ inch squares

2 green onions, sliced

- Pour water into large pot; add miso.
- Bring to a boil while stirring constantly.
- When miso is blended, reduce heat to simmer.
- Taste; add more miso if saltier taste is preferred.
- Add tofu and cook 5 minutes.
- Top each bowl of soup with green onions.

Serves 4

*Miso is a fermented soybean paste found in the Asian section of the grocery store. It lasts for a long time in the refrigerator.

Gazpacho

Cool summer soup

2-3 tomatoes, diced

2 medium red bell peppers, diced

2 medium cucumbers, peeled, seeded, and diced

½ cup onion, chopped

2 tbsp lime juice

2 cups V-8™ juice

2 tbsp cilantro, chopped

Hot sauce to taste

Lime slices optional

- Combine all ingredients in a large bowl or pitcher; chill for at least 1 hour.
- Serve in bowls or mugs garnished with lime slices.

Serves 4

Shrimp "Ceviche"

"Ceviche"

1 large or 2 medium Roma tomatoes, diced

1 large cucumber, peeled, seeded, and diced

½ cup red onion, diced

¼ cup fresh cilantro, chopped

1-2 tbsp jalapeno, seeded and minced *(optional)*

2 tbsp olive oil

1 tsp salt

2 dashes hot sauce

1 lb shrimp, cooked and peeled

Lime slices

Marinade

1 cup orange juice

⅓ cup lime juice

¼ cup ketchup

3 cloves garlic, minced

- Combine the marinade ingredients. Set aside.
- Lightly toss the remaining ingredients in a large bowl.
- Pour the marinade over the top and gently stir.
- Chill.
- Serve cold in wine or martini glasses with a spoon. Garnish with lime slices.

Serves 6-8

FYI: "Ceviche" is a process of "cooking" seafood by contact with the acids in citrus juices. You may use raw shrimp in this recipe, if desired; however, it is necessary to marinade overnight to "cook".

Tuscan Meatball Soup

1 cup onion, chopped

3-4 cloves garlic, minced

½ cup olive oil

4 cups chicken broth

2 cans Great Northern beans, drained

One 28 oz can petite diced tomatoes

¼ cup lemon juice

1 tbsp sun-dried tomatoes *(not packed in oil)*, chopped

2 cups frozen Italian style meatballs *(more if desired)*

1 lb pkg fresh baby spinach

Freshly grated Parmesan cheese

- In a soup pot, sauté the garlic and onions in the olive oil.
- Carefully, add the chicken broth, beans, petite diced tomatoes, lemon juice, and sun-dried tomatoes. Bring to a boil, then reduce heat to medium.
- Add meatballs and heat through.
- Just before serving, stir in the spinach and wilt.
- Top each bowl with Parmesan cheese.

Serves 4-6

Shortcut Brunswick Stew

3 chicken breasts with ribs and skin

1 strip bacon (optional)

1 packet dried Lipton Noodle Soup™ mix

One 28 oz can petite diced tomatoes

1 cup canned lima beans, rinsed and drained

One 12 oz can shoepeg corn, drained

- Place chicken breast and bacon in a soup pot and just barely cover with water. Bring water to a boil, reduce heat and simmer for 40 minutes.
- Remove chicken to a plate and discard bacon. Cool chicken, then shred into bite-sized pieces.
- Add tomatoes and juice to broth. Bring to a boil and add packet of noodle soup. Boil for 5 minutes.
- Lower heat to a simmer; add lima beans, corn, and chicken.
- Simmer for at least 30 more minutes.

Serves 4-6

Chicken and Dumplings

3 chicken breasts with ribs and skin

One 10¾ oz can cream of chicken soup

4 tbsp butter

2 tbsp flour

1 can buttermilk biscuits (not flaky)

- Cook chicken in just enough water to cover in a large soup pot.*

- Bring to a boil, cover and simmer for 40 minutes.

- Remove chicken breast to a plate to cool.

- Strain broth into another pot.

- Melt butter in original pot. Stir in flour and slowly whisk in 2 cups of the chicken broth. (If you pour in too much liquid at a time, you will get lumps.)

- Whisk in cream of chicken soup and then 2 more cups of chicken broth.

- Shred cooled chicken. Add to sauce and simmer until sauce thickens.

- Pinch pieces of the biscuit dough, mash between thumb and forefinger and drop into the boiling sauce.

- Reduce heat, cover and cook for 15 minutes.

- Stir often as sauce continues to thicken and tends to stick to the bottom of the pot. Add more chicken broth as needed.

Serves 4-6

*FYI: This technique creates a richer broth. Too much water results in weaker broth.

Rosemary Vegetable Soup

1 cup water

1 tbsp olive oil

2 leeks *(white part)*, chopped

1 medium onion, chopped

½ tsp thyme

½ tsp rosemary

1 clove garlic, minced

3 cups chicken broth

One 28 oz can petite diced tomatoes, undrained

1 tbsp tomato paste

2 cups red potatoes, cut into cubes

½ cup carrots, sliced

½ cup celery, chopped

1 cup kale, shredded

Salt and pepper to taste

- In a soup pot, bring water and olive oil to a boil. Add leeks and onions and simmer for 5 minutes.
- Add thyme, rosemary, and garlic and cook for another 5 minutes.
- Add chicken broth, tomatoes, and tomato paste. Bring to a boil.
- Add potatoes, carrots, and celery and return to a boil. Reduce heat and simmer for an hour.
- Five minutes before serving, stir in kale. Add salt and pepper to taste.

Serves 6-8

Basic Bowl of Greens

2 cups Romaine lettuce, washed and torn

2 cups baby spinach, washed

¼ cup onion, chopped

- Combine greens and chopped onion.
- Top with your choice of cooked meats and seafoods, nuts, vegetables, fruits, and dressing.

Basic Olive Oil Dressing
Great alone or to embellish with herbs and spices

¼ cup lemon juice or ¼ cup balsamic vinegar

¼ cup olive oil

¼ tsp black pepper *(preferably ground)*

½ tsp salt

- Combine all of the above ingredients. No need to refrigerate. Add various spices to create different dressings.

Caprese Salad
Pretty on a summer buffet table

1 cup pine nuts

1 tbsp olive oil

½ lb fresh Mozzarella cheese, sliced into ¼" – ½" rounds

2 large tomatoes, thinly sliced *(try alternating red and yellow tomatoes for extra color)*

16 fresh basil leaves, cut into thin strips

4-5 tbsp olive oil

- Lightly brown the pine nuts in 1 tablespoon olive oil. Do not drain.
- On a large serving platter, alternate the tomato and cheese slices.
- Top with strips of basil.
- Pour the sautéed pine nuts and oil over the tomatoes and cheese.
- Drizzle the remaining oil over the salad.

Serves 4

Greek Slaw

1 small head of cabbage, washed, drained, and sliced into slivers *(or purchase precut bag)* *

½ sweet onion, thinly sliced

1 cup grape tomatoes, halved

1 cucumber, peeled and thinly sliced

1 green and/or red or yellow bell pepper, cut into thin strips

1 cup Kalamata olives, pitted

4 oz crumbled feta cheese

Dressing

⅔ cup extra virgin olive oil

⅓ cup rice vinegar

2 cloves garlic, minced

1 tsp ground cumin

½ tsp salt

½ tsp pepper

- Combine dressing ingredients in a jar and set aside.
- Layer *(preferably in a glass bowl)* the remaining ingredients, beginning with the cabbage
- Vigorously shake dressing and pour over the salad.
- Refrigerate at least 6 hours to overnight.
- Toss before serving.

Serves 8-10

* **FYI:** Washing Cabbage: Remove the outer leaves of the cabbage, then cut in half and remove core. Rinse each half and drain well.

Marinated Cucumber and Onion Salad

1 medium white onion, sliced into thin rings

2 large cucumbers, peeled and sliced thin

1 tsp black pepper

1 tbsp salt

½ cup white vinegar

½ cup sugar

1 tbsp dill weed

- Mix salt, pepper, sugar and dill weed in a small bowl until the sugar dissolves.
- Pour over the sliced vegetables and chill for at least 3 hours or overnight.
- Toss and serve with a slotted spoon.

Serves 4-6

Artichoke/Tomato Insalata

Best when tomatoes are in season

8 large Romaine lettuce leaves

Balsamic vinaigrette salad dressing

One 14 oz can artichoke hearts, drained and quartered

2 large tomatoes, cut into wedges

1 tsp basil

One 3.8 oz can Spanish olives, sliced and drained

- Gently mix tomatoes, artichoke hearts, olives, and basil in a medium bowl; refrigerate.
- When ready to serve, gently toss tomato mixture with dressing and place on lettuce leaves on individual salad plates.

Serves 4

Twenty-Two Second Cole Slaw

One 16 oz pkg prepared slaw mix

One 10 oz pkg frozen baby peas, thawed and drained

½ cup pecans, chopped

Dressing

½ cup canola or vegetable oil

¼ cup sugar

1 tbsp poppy seeds

1 tsp salt

¼ cup white vinegar

- Mix dressing in the bottom of a large serving bowl.
- Toss the slaw into the serving bowl with dressing, peas, and pecans. Serve immediately.

Serves 6-8

Confetti Salad
Great for picnics and tailgates

One 15 oz can petite peas, drained

One 14 oz can shoepeg corn, drained

One 15 oz Blue Lake French cut green beans, drained

One 4 oz jar chopped pimento, drained OR 1 red bell pepper, chopped

1 green bell pepper, chopped

1 cup celery, chopped

2 small green onions, sliced

Dressing

¾ cup sugar

½ cup vegetable oil

½ cup apple cider vinegar

¼ tsp each, salt and pepper

½ tsp dry mustard

½ tsp dried basil

- In a medium saucepan, cook the dressing ingredients over a medium heat until the sugar dissolves. Cool for 30 minutes.
- Place all vegetables into a large bowl.
- Pour cooled dressing over vegetables and chill overnight.
- Serve with slotted spoon.

Serves 12

Mandarin Orange Salad

½ cup pecan pieces

1 tbsp sugar

1 head Romaine lettuce, torn into bite-size pieces

1 cup celery, chopped

2 green onions

1 cup Mandarin oranges, drained and chilled

Dressing

½ tsp salt

¼ tsp pepper

½ tsp Tabasco™ sauce

1 tbsp sugar

¼ tsp tarragon

¼ cup apple cider vinegar

¾ cup vegetable oil

- In a small frying pan cook pecans in sugar over a low heat, stirring constantly *(watch carefully as they burn easily)*.
- When sugar has melted over pecans, place on waxed paper to cool.
- Place lettuce, celery, and onions in a salad bowl, cover and refrigerate.
- Mix dressing ingredients and refrigerate until serving time.
- Before serving, add Mandarin oranges to salad bowl, toss with dressing, and sprinkle with pecans.

Serves 4

Baby Spinach and Strawberry Salad

Two 6 oz bags baby spinach, washed, drained, and torn into bite-size pieces

1 pint fresh strawberries, washed, hulled, and sliced

Bleu cheese *(optional)*

Walnuts *(optional)*

Dressing*

½ cup sugar

1 tbsp poppy seeds

½ cup apple cider vinegar

1 tsp onion, minced

¼ tsp Worcestershire sauce

¼ tsp paprika

½ cup vegetable oil

- Mix dressing ingredients together in a small jar.
- When ready to serve, gently toss all ingredients together.

Serves 8

* Bottled Bleu Cheese and Raspberry Vinaigrettes are good options for this salad.

Thai Noodle Salad

1 lb box thin spaghetti

½ cup soy sauce

3 tbsp roasted sesame seeds

⅓ cup vegetable oil

1 tbsp sugar

1 tsp ground ginger

1 tbsp rice vinegar

3-4 tbsp crunchy peanut butter

¼ tsp ground red pepper

¼ cup green onions, sliced

- Cook pasta according to package directions; cool.
- Mix the remaining ingredients in a medium bowl until well blended.
- Toss well with the noodles.
- Chill for at least 3 hours.

Serves 6-8

Tabbouleh Salad

Salad

1 cup cracked whole grain bulghur wheat *(bulghur wheat is found in the health food or Middle-Eastern section of the grocery store)*

1 bunch parsley, finely chopped

1 bunch green onions, sliced

1-2 cups tomatoes, diced

2 large cucumbers, peeled, seeded, and diced*

Dressing

½ cup lemon juice

2 tsp salt

½ tsp black pepper

½ cup olive oil

- Mix salad ingredients together in a large bowl.
- Combine dressing ingredients in a jar and shake well.
- Pour dressing over salad, toss, and refrigerate for at least 2 hours while the wheat softens and expands.
- Toss again before serving.

Serves 8-10

FYI: Keeps in the refrigerator for 3 days.

* FYI: To seed cucumbers: Peel and slice in half. Drag a spoon down the center removing seeds.

Red Potato Salad

3 lbs medium red potatoes, washed

1½ tbsp olive oil

3 leeks (white parts only), washed and coarsely chopped*

¾ cup green onions, chopped

½ cup fresh parsley, chopped

½ cup mayonnaise

3 tbsp white wine vinegar

1 tbsp Dijon mustard

¼ tsp dried tarragon

Salt and pepper to taste

- Place potatoes in a large pot and cover with water.
- Bring to boil, then reduce heat and simmer for 30 minutes or until potatoes are tender *(knife goes easily into potato when done)*.
- Drain potatoes into a colander and cool.
- When cool to touch, slice potatoes ¼" thick and set aside.
- Heat olive oil over a medium heat in a 12" skillet and sauté leeks for 5 minutes.
- In a large serving bowl, mix the mayonnaise, vinegar, mustard, tarragon, salt, and pepper together with a whisk or fork.
- Add the sliced potatoes, leeks, green onions, and parsley.
- Toss well and refrigerate.

Serves 10-12

*FYI: Cut leeks in half lengthwise to wash. Dirt tends to adhere to the inside of the stalks.

Salmon Salad

1 cup cooked salmon, cut into 2" pieces

2 green onions, sliced

2 cups fresh spinach, loosely packed and torn into bite-sized pieces

2 cups Romaine lettuce, torn into bite-sized pieces

1 cup grape tomatoes, halved

- Toss together and top with lemon dressing* before serving.

Serves 4

*Lemon Dressing

¼ cup freshly squeezed lemon juice

¼ cup olive oil

¼ tsp black pepper or Krazy Pepper™

½ tsp salt

- Whisk together until salt is dissolved and pour over salad.

Thai Chicken Salad

Vinaigrette

½ cup olive oil

1 cup rice vinegar

⅓ cup soy sauce

2-3 cloves garlic, minced

2 tbsp hot chili oil

Salad

2½ to 3 lbs boneless, skinless chicken breast, boiled and shredded

½ medium red onion, diced

¼ cup fresh basil, chopped

1 bunch green onions, sliced

½ cup fresh cilantro, chopped

1 cup salted peanuts, chopped

- Combine vinaigrette ingredients in a jar. Set aside.
- Place chicken in a large bowl with onions, basil, and cilantro.
- Toss with vinaigrette and refrigerate for at least 3 hours.
- Mix in peanuts just before serving.
- Serve alone on a bed of lettuce, or stuffed in a pita pocket.

Serves 4-6

Cranberry-Walnut Chicken Salad

2 loosely packed cups of fresh spinach, washed and torn into bite-size pieces

2 loosely packed cups of fresh Romaine, washed and torn into bite-size pieces

2 green onions, chopped

1 cup walnuts, chopped

½ cup dried cranberries

2 pre-cooked chicken breasts, shredded

1 cup feta cheese, crumbled

Dressing

¼ cup lemon juice

¼ cup olive oil

¼ tsp pepper

½ tsp salt

- Combine dressing ingredients in a jar, set aside.
- Toss spinach, Romaine lettuce, onions, walnuts, cranberries, chicken, and feta with the dressing.

Serves 4-6

FYI: Make Ahead of Time!

Refrigerate the spinach, lettuce, and onion together in a plastic zippered bag.

Place the remaining ingredients in separate sandwich bags. Toss together with

the dressing when ready to serve.

Chinese Chicken Salad

4-6 boneless chicken breast, or 1 whole chicken, cooked and shredded
(can use baked deli chicken)

1 head iceberg lettuce or ½ head romaine plus ½ bunch
of spinach, shredded

4 green onions, sliced

2 tbsp sliced almonds

2 tbsp sesame seeds

Dressing

2 tbsp sugar

1 tsp salt

½ tsp black pepper

¼ cup vegetable or canola oil

1 tbsp sesame oil

3 tbsp rice vinegar

- Stir-fry the sesame seeds and almonds together in a small fry pan over medium-high heat until brown. (The seeds and almonds contain oil, so additional oil is not necessary.)
- Set aside to cool on a paper towel.
- Combine dressing ingredients in a small jar or bowl.
- Toss chicken, almonds, sesame seeds, salad ingredients, and dressing together just before serving to ensure that the greens remain crisp.

Serves 4-6

Margarit's Mexican Salad

Topping

1 lb ground beef

1 tbsp vegetable oil

½ large onion, chopped

One 15.5 oz can red kidney beans, rinsed and drained

¼ cup Catalina dressing

½ cup water

1 tbsp chili powder

Tabasco™ *(optional)*

Salad

4 cups lettuce shredded

2 medium tomatoes, diced

½ cup onions, chopped

8 oz cheddar cheese, grated

- Brown the beef and onion in the oil, drain.
- Stir in beans, dressing, water, and chili powder and simmer for 15 minutes.
- Crumble the tortilla chips in the bottom of 4 bowls, then layer the lettuce, tomatoes, onion, and topping. Top with desired amount of grated cheese.

Serves 4

Cranberry Relish Salad
A holiday favorite!

2 cups fresh cranberries, washed and drained

1 firm orange *(including peel)*, washed and seeds removed

1 firm lemon *(including peel)*, washed and seeds removed

1 cup sugar

Two 3 oz pkgs of cranberry or orange flavored JELL-O™

2 cups water

1 cup celery, diced small

1 cup nuts, chopped

- Chop the fruits by hand, food processor, or blender into small pieces, reserving as much of the juice as possible.
- Place into a medium size bowl and add the sugar. Mix well, cover, and chill for 1 hour.
- Remove from the refrigerator, drain and save the liquid.
- Empty the fruit into a large serving bowl.
- Add the 2 pkgs of JELL-O™ with 2 cups of boiling water, stirring in the reserved fruit juices.
- Chill until firm.
- When thickened, stir in celery and nuts.
- Keep refrigerated until serving.

Serves 8-10

Entrées

Entrées

The entrée, while the focal point of the meal, doesn't have to be difficult to prepare. Entrees can range from a hardy salad to a baked chicken and pasta dish. Follow our tips to insure that your main attraction will have your guests asking for a second showing!

Tips:

- Consider the NUMBER OF PEOPLE you are feeding. Choose your entrée based on amount needed, convenience, and price. For example, when feeding a crowd, pick an entrée such as Spaghetti. The sauce is easy to prepare ahead of time and the pasta will stretch the sauce and your dollar! An entrée such as Shrimp Scampi would be more reasonable for a small dinner party for four.

- Consider the SEASON. Heavier entrees such as roasts and chili are comfort food in the fall and winter; lighter fare such as salads and grilled items work well in the spring and summer.

- Consider the OCCASION. Special occasions like birthdays and graduation celebrations may warrant a more elegant entrée such as pork tenderloin, while outdoor summer dining may call for fajitas.

Food in a Flash! **Entrées**

Pick up one of the following prepared entrées and add an easy-to-prepare

vegetable such as frozen broccoli or a bagged salad mix to complete your meal.

Grocery Store Entrées:
Deli section
Rotisserie chicken
Barbeque chicken, pork, or beef
Ribs
Fried chicken pieces or strips
Chicken salad

Refrigerated section
Frozen pasta entrées- lasagna, tortellini, stuffed shells
(served with a prepared spaghetti sauce)
Cooked shrimp
Smoked salmon

Restaurants:
Most restaurants are happy to sell you any entrée to take home.

Marinated Flank Steak

One 1½-2 lb flank steak

¼ cup olive oil

¼ cup red wine

¼ cup soy sauce

2 cloves garlic, minced

- Score the flank steak on both sides and place in a one gallon zippered bag.*
- Whisk together olive oil, wine, soy sauce, and garlic and pour over steak.
- Zip closed and flip bag to completely cover the steak with marinade.
- Refrigerate 8 hours to overnight.
- Grill over hot coals, 7 minutes on each side for a rare steak.
- Slice thinly on a diagonal for maximum tenderness.

Serves 4-6

To Score meat: gently cut diagonal lines (\\\\) about 1 inch apart along one side of the meat. Then cut lines in the opposite direction (////) to make "diamonds." Do this lightly on both sides of the meat. Do not cut through the meat. This will help the marinade to penetrate and keep the meat from "curling."

Encore:

Flank steak sandwiches

Steak fajitas

Steak salad

Beef and Broccoli Stir-fry

Encore: Flank Steak Sandwiches

Flank steak, cooked and sliced

Dijon mustard

Swiss cheese

English muffins, split

A.1.™ Steak Sauce

- Preheat broiler.
- Lightly toast English muffins on a cookie sheet.
- Spread with mustard and steak sauce.
- Top with steak and cheese.
- Broil until cheese melts.

Encore: Steak Fajitas

Flank steak, cooked and sliced

Green pepper, slivered

Tortillas

Onion, silvered

Canola oil

- Sauté onions and peppers in a small amount of oil in a skillet.
- Add flank steak until heated through.
- Wrap tortillas in a damp paper towel and heat in microwave for one minute.
- Add steak and peppers to the warm tortillas along with favorite toppings.

Encore: Steak Salad

Flank steak, cooked and sliced

Blue Cheese Dressing

Basic Bowl of Greens *(see recipe)*

- Place cooked steak on top of greens and top with dressing.

Encore: Beef and Broccoli Stir-fry

2 cups sirloin or flank steak cut into thin strips *(or use left-over cooked beef)*

1 medium onion, cut into slivers

1 tsp hot chili-garlic sauce*

¼ cup cooking oil

2 cups fresh broccoli, sliced at an angle into bite-sized pieces

Cooked rice

- Place broccoli in a medium bowl; add ¼ cup water, cover, and microwave on high for 3 minutes. Drain thoroughly.
- Place the sliced onion and broccoli on a cookie sheet or platter and set aside.**
- In a large skillet, heat the oil to medium-high heat and quickly cook the steak slices, stirring constantly. *(If using left-over steak, add later with the chili-garlic sauce.)*
- Remove the steak and quickly add the broccoli and onion.
- Cook 1 minute and add the steak and chili-garlic sauce, tossing gently.
- Serve over rice.

Serves 2-4 (depending on how much left-over steak you have)

* Hot chili-garlic sauce is a very hot and spicy sauce found in the Asian section of the grocery store. Use sparingly.

** Stir-frying works best if all ingredients are close at hand and ready to add quickly.

Nana's Sunday Pot Roast

2 lb sirloin tip roast

½ cup flour

1 tsp dried parsley

1 tsp seasoned salt

2 tbsp vegetable oil

1 packet dried Lipton Onion Soup™ mix

One 10¾ oz can cream of mushroom soup

1 soup can water

2 cups baby carrots

1 large onion, quartered

3 russet potatoes, peeled, and quartered

- Preheat over to 350°F
- Mix flour, parsley, and seasoned salt in a shallow dish.
- Rub mixture over the entire roast.
- In a small bowl, combine packet of soup mix, can of soup, and water. Set aside.
- Heat oil in a large pot over medium high heat. Brown the roast on all sides.
- Carefully pour the soup mixture over the roast.
- Cover and bake in preheated oven for 1½ hours.
- Remove pot from oven and add carrots, onion and potatoes.
- Place back in oven and cook for another hour. Adjust the cooking time for a larger roast. *(Check with fork to see if potatoes and beef are tender.)*
- Remove roast to a plate and let sit for 10 minutes before serving. Roast should tear easily with a fork or can be sliced.

Serves 4

Meatloaf

1½ lbs ground beef

¼ cup onion, diced

½ cup ketchup

¼ cup bread crumbs

1 egg

1 tbsp Worcestershire sauce

½ tsp pepper

1 slice of bacon

Sauce:
½ cup ketchup
2 tbsp brown sugar
1 tbsp Dijon mustard

- Preheat oven to 350°F.

- In a large bowl, mix together *(with hands)* beef, onion, ketchup, bread crumbs, egg, Worcestershire sauce, and pepper.

- Mold into a loaf creating an edge on top to hold in the sauce that will be added later. Top with the bacon slice and place into a small roasting pan.

- Mix sauce ingredients together and set aside.

- Bake meatloaf for 25 minutes, remove from oven, pour fat off and top with sauce.

- Continue baking for 20 more minutes.

Serves 6

Encore: Meatloaf Sandwiches

Meatloaf, cooked and sliced

Italian bread

Condiments of choice: ketchup, mayonnaise, lettuce, tomato, cheese, onion, steak sauce.

Meatballs

1½ lbs ground chuck	¼ cup bread crumbs
1 tbsp parsley	½ tsp garlic salt
1 egg	Pepper

- Preheat oven to 350°F.
- In a large bowl, mix all ingredients together,
  (your hands work best for mixing)
- Pinch off small amounts of mixture and roll into 1½" balls.
- Let brown in the oven for about 30 minutes.
- Drain on paper towels.

Makes about 20 meatballs

Encore: Meatball Sandwiches

Meatballs, cooked

Sub rolls

Jar of spaghetti sauce or homemade sauce

Mozzarella cheese

- Pour sauce over meatballs in a fry pan. Cook on medium-low heat until meatballs are heated through.
- Spoon meatballs and sauce into sub rolls.
- Top with cheese.
- Place on microwave-safe plate and heat for about one minute or just until cheese melts.

Spaghetti

2 tbsp olive oil

1 lb Italian sausage, casings removed or ground Italian sausage

One 28 oz can petite diced tomatoes

One 14 oz can tomato sauce

One small can tomato paste

1 small onion, cut into slivers

½ tsp crushed red pepper

2 cloves garlic, diced

1 tsp sugar

2 tsp dried basil

1 lb box spaghetti, cooked and drained

- In a large pot, brown and crumble sausage in oil over medium-high heat. Drain.
- Add remaining ingredients and simmer for at least an hour.
- Ladle over cooked pasta.

Serves 6

Chef Mike's Spaghetti Sauce

A thinner, sweeter sauce

½ lb sweet Italian sausage *(casings removed)*

1 lb ground chuck

2 tbsp olive oil

2 medium onions, chopped

1 large green bell pepper, chopped

2 cloves garlic, minced

Two 16 oz cans of diced tomatoes

Five 16 oz cans tomato sauce

2 tbsp sugar

2 tsp basil

1 tsp crushed red pepper

Cooked pasta

- Heat olive oil in a large sauce pan over medium heat.
- Brown the sausage and ground chuck in the olive oil, crumbling with a fork or spatula.
- Pour the cooked meats in a colander to drain, reserving 2 tbsp of oil in the large saucepot.
- Sauté the green pepper and onion in the oil until tender. Add tomatoes, tomato sauce, and spices. Simmer for at least 1 hour.
- Serve over cooked pasta.

Serves 10-12

Optional: Add meatballs for an extra hardy meal!

Sauce Encore:

Use leftover sauce on the following

Meatball sandwiches

Lasagna

Italian sausage sandwiches

Encore: Italian Sausage Sandwiches

1 lb pkg Italian sausage *(mild or hot)*

1 green pepper, sliced into strips

1 medium onion, sliced into slivers

1 tbsp olive oil

One 26 oz jar of spaghetti sauce *(or leftover sauce)*

1 cup Mozzarella cheese

5 hoagie or sub buns

- Brown the sausage links in olive oil over medium heat in a 12" skillet.
- Reduce the heat to low, cover and let cook for 15 minutes. Remove from skillet. Drain all but 2 tbsp of fat.
- In the same skillet, add the green pepper and onion; sauté until tender. Stir in spaghetti sauce, add sausage, cover and simmer for 15 more minutes.
- Cut a "V" through the length of the buns making space for the sausage. Place a sausage and sauce in each bun. Sprinkle with Mozzarella cheese.
- Place on a microwave safe plate and microwave until the cheese melts.

Serves 5

Lasagna *(May assemble ahead of time)*

1 egg

One 16 oz container ricotta cheese

2 cups Mozzarella cheese, shredded *(reserve 1/2 c. for topping)*

¼ cup Parmesan cheese

One 26 oz jar spaghetti sauce or leftover sauce

One 9 oz pkg no-boil lasagna noodles

- Preheat oven to 350°
- Combine egg and cheeses in a small bowl, reserving ½ cup Mozzarella cheese. Set aside.
- Spread a thin layer of sauce on the bottom of a 9"x 13" baking dish.
- Start layering. Begin with a layer of noodles, egg mixture, sauce. Repeat. Top with ½ cup of Mozzarella cheese.
- Cover with foil and bake for 30 minutes. Remove foil and bake an additional 15 minutes.

Serves 6

Becki's Spinach Lasagna

(Can be assembled ahead of time and refrigerated until ready to bake)

Spray oil

One 10 oz box frozen, chopped spinach

2 eggs

2 cups grated Mozzarella cheese, divided

One 24 oz carton cottage cheese

½ cup grated Parmesan cheese

½ tsp dried oregano

2 tsp dried basil

¼ tsp crushed red pepper

One 9 oz box of no-boil lasagna noodles

One 26 oz jar of spaghetti sauce

- Preheat oven to 350°F. Grease a 9"x13" casserole dish.
- Thaw the spinach in a colander and squeeze the liquid out by hand.
- Stir together the spinach, eggs, 1½ cups Mozzarella, Parmesan, cottage cheese, oregano, basil, and red pepper in a large bowl.
- Pour a thin layer of spaghetti sauce on the bottom of the casserole dish. Cover the sauce with a layer of the no-boil lasagna noodles, then add a layer of the spinach-cheese mixture. Continue layering in this order, topping off with a thin layer of spaghetti sauce.
- Sprinkle the remaining ½ cup of Mozzarella cheese on the very top of the casserole. Cover with foil.
- Bake covered for 1 hour. Uncover and bake for an additional 15 minutes.

Serves 8-10

Chicken Linguine with Feta and Tomatoes

6 boneless, skinless chicken breasts

2 tbsp olive oil, divided

One 28 oz can petite diced tomatoes, undrained

1 medium onion, sliced into thin rings

1½ tsp dried oregano or Italian seasoning

1 tsp garlic, minced

1 cup crumbled feta cheese

One 1 lb box of linguine, cooked according to pkg directions

- Preheat oven to 350°
- Lay chicken breasts in a 9"x13" baking pan coated with 1 tbsp of the olive oil.
- Sprinkle chicken with oregano and garlic; top with onion rings and tomatoes.
- Drizzle with remaining tbsp of olive oil and top with feta cheese.
- Bake for 1 hour.
- Serve over cooked linguine.

Serves 4

Tomato/Italian Sausage/Broccoli Pasta

2 tbsp olive oil

1 small onion, chopped

2 cloves garlic, minced

2 lbs Roma tomatoes, chopped

2 tbsp olive oil

1 lb hot Italian sausage

Penne pasta

2 cups frozen broccoli florets

Freshly grated Parmesan

- Saute onion in olive oil in a 12" skillet until tender.
- Stir in garlic; add tomatoes. Cook on medium heat for 10 minutes.
- In a separate skillet and over medium-high heat, brown the links of Italian sausage in the other 2 tbsp olive oil. When brown on all sides, turn heat to low, cover and let cook through.
- Slice the sausage and add to the tomatoes.
- Bring a pot of water to boiling and cook pasta for about 5 minutes.
- When pasta is almost ready *(bite a piece to check)*, add broccoli florets to the boiling water.
- Cook until pasta is ready. Drain.
- Spoon tomato/sausage sauce over pasta and broccoli.
- Sprinkle with Parmesan.

Serves: 4-6

Linguine with Creamy Tomato Sauce

1 medium onion, chopped

1 garlic clove, minced

1 tbsp olive oil

One 14 oz can Italian style tomatoes, diced

1 tbsp basil

¾ tsp sugar

¼ tsp oregano

½ cup whipping cream

1 tbsp butter

8 oz linguine, cooked and drained

Salt and pepper to taste

Parmesan cheese

- Sauté onion and garlic in a large fry pan over medium heat.
- Stir in tomatoes with juice, basil, sugar, oregano, salt and pepper.
- Bring mixture to a boil until most of the liquid evaporates.
- Remove from heat; stir in whipping cream and butter.
- Place on low heat just until heated through.
- Serve over cooked linguine.
- Sprinkle with Parmesan cheese.

Serves 4

Greek Style Pasta

1 lb box of pasta *(penne, bowtie, or rotini)*

One 10 oz pkg frozen chopped spinach

2 tbsp extra virgin olive oil

1 medium onion, diced

6 cloves garlic, minced

1 cup feta cheese *(or more)*

Salt and pepper

- Cook pasta according to package directions. Set aside.
- Defrost spinach in microwave; drain and squeeze dry.
- Sauté onion and garlic in olive oil over medium heat until translucent.
- Add pasta, then spinach. *(More olive oil may be required to disperse spinach into the pasta.)*
- Salt and pepper to taste.
- Toss with feta cheese just before serving.

Serves 4-6

Curried Lentils

1 lb dried lentils, sorted and rinsed*

One 14½ oz can chicken broth

1 tbsp curry powder

Salt to taste

Rice, cooked

Plain yogurt

- In a large pot, pour chicken broth over lentils and add enough water to cover.
- Bring to a boil; stir in curry and salt.
- Reduce heat to low; cover and simmer for 20-30 minutes until lentils are tender.
- Serve over rice and top with plain yogurt.

Serves 4-6

*FYI: Bags of dried beans and peas sometimes have small stones and other debris. Sort and rinse.

Variations: Can add chicken and leftover vegetables.

Roasted Turkey
Easier than you think.

- Preheat oven to 325°F.

- Rinse the outside and inside of the turkey and pat dry.

- Place turkey in a shallow baking pan and rub skin with oil or butter.

- Sprinkle with salt and pepper.

- Place the pan in the center of the oven and bake as directed on the time table on the wrapper. **The Safest Way To Insure That The Turkey Is Cooked Is To Use A Meat Thermometer.**

- When the turkey is golden brown, loosely cover with a piece of aluminum foil *(this keeps the skin from turning dark brown)*.

- When the turkey is cooked, remove from oven and let "rest" for about 20 minutes to redistribute juices and make it easier to carve.

Turkey Tips:

- Turkeys are purchased fresh or frozen. If buying fresh, pay attention to the expiration date. If frozen, read and follow instructions on wrapper for thawing.

- Buy approximately ¼ - 1 lb per serving.
(Don't forget to allow for all the delicious turkey leftovers!)

- Consider buying a turkey breast if you only like white meat.

- Turkeys usually have internal organs *(gizzards, heart, liver)* wrapped in plastic and stuffed into two different cavities. **Be Sure And Remove These Before Baking.**

Encore:

Stovetop Turkey Hash

Turkey Tetrazzini

Turkey Sandwiches

Encore: **Stovetop Turkey Hash**

1 large potato, peeled and cut into ¼" slices

1 small onion, thinly sliced

Water

3 cups cooked turkey, sliced

1 envelope McCormick Brown Gravy™ mix

1½ cups water

- Layer the potato slices, then top with onion slices in a 12" skillet.

- Add just enough water to the skillet to barely cover the onions.

- Cook over medium heat until the potatoes are tender *(about 8-10 minutes-check to make sure the potatoes aren't sticking to the bottom of the pan. If sticking, add a little more water.)*

- While potatoes are cooking, pour the gravy mix into a small bowl and slowly stir in the 1½ cups of water.

- Add turkey to the potatoes and onions. Pour the gravy over the turkey.

- Use a spatula to gently mix the gravy into the turkey and potatoes.

- The dish is ready when the gravy thickens and the mixture is heated through.

- Add salt and pepper to taste before serving.

Serves 2

Encore: Turkey Tetrazzini

Can also be made with chicken

4 tbsp butter	4 tbsp flour
4 oz mushrooms, sliced	Spray oil
½ cup onion, chopped	7 oz spaghetti, cooked and drained
2 cups chicken broth	1 cup half-n-half
¼ cup plus 1 tbsp Parmesan cheese	1 tbsp sherry

2 cups turkey (or chicken), cooked and shredded

- Preheat oven to 350°F.
- Sauté mushrooms and onion in butter in a medium saucepan.
- Stir in flour; slowly whisk in chicken broth until sauce is smooth.
- Bring just to a boil and simmer until sauce thickens.
- Whisk in half-n-half; cook for 3 minutes.
- Stir in Parmesan and sherry.
- Put cooked spaghetti in greased 9"x13" casserole dish.
- Top with turkey then cover with sauce.
- Sprinkle with remaining tablespoon of Parmesan.
- Bake for 30 minutes or until cooked through.

Serves 6

Encore: Turkey Sandwiches

Leftover sliced turkey

Sandwich bread

Condiments of choice: mayonnaise, lettuce, tomato, onion, cranberry sauce

Oven Baked Chicken Breasts

4 boneless, skinless chicken breasts

1 cup breadcrumbs

¼ cup Parmesan cheese

1 tsp oregano

1 tsp basil

Garlic salt to taste

½ cup melted butter

- Preheat oven to 350°F.
- Combine breadcrumbs, Parmesan cheese, oregano, basil, and garlic salt in a small bowl.
- Dip the breast in the melted butter and then dredge in breadcrumb mixture.
- Place in a lightly greased 9" x 13" casserole dish and bake uncovered for 40 minutes.

Serves 2-4

Aloha Chicken

Dinner in one pan

1 lb boneless, skinless chicken breast

2 tbsp butter

1 clove garlic, minced

1 cup green pepper, thinly sliced

1 cup carrots, chopped

¼ cup soy sauce

3 tbsp brown sugar

3 tbsp apple cider vinegar

1 cup chicken broth

½ tsp ground ginger

1 small can pineapple chunks, drain and reserve liquid

2 cups instant rice *(white or brown)*

- Mix soy sauce, brown sugar, chicken broth, vinegar, ginger, and pineapple juice together in a medium bowl. Set aside.
- Slice the chicken breasts into thin strips. Brown chicken, a handful at a time, in melted butter in a 12" fry pan. Remove browned strips to a separate bowl until all the chicken is lightly browned. (*More butter may be needed.*)
- Add garlic, green pepper, and carrots to remaining butter and sauté until tender.
- Add pineapple, heating through, then return chicken to the pan.
- Stir in soy sauce mixture.
- Pour in rice. Cover. Reduce heat to low and cook for 15-20 minutes or until the liquid is absorbed and the rice is fluffy.
- Stir before serving.

Serves 4

Cornish Hens

Two 1 lb Cornish hens

Melted butter or vegetable oil

Salt and pepper

- Preheat oven to 400°F.
- Rinse the hens inside and out and blot with a paper towel.
- Brush the hens with butter or oil.
- Sprinkle with salt and pepper.
- Bake at 400°F for 15 minutes to brown.
- Reduce heat to 350°F and bake for 45 more minutes.

Serves 2

Note: Cornish hens, like turkeys, and sometimes whole chickens, often have livers and gizzards wrapped in paper or plastic in the inside cavity for use in gravies and dressings. Be sure to check for these and remove before cooking.

Chicken Breasts Stuffed with Goat Cheese and Sun-dried Tomatoes

4 boneless, skinless chicken breasts

5.5 oz goat cheese

2 tbsp sun-dried tomatoes packed in oil

1 tsp dried basil

Salt and pepper to taste

2 tbsp extra virgin olive oil

- Preheat oven to 350°F.
- Cut a horizontal slit through each chicken breast to create a pocket.
- Combine cheese, tomatoes, basil, salt and pepper in a medium bowl.
- Stuff approximately 2 tablespoons of the mixture into each breast and secure with toothpicks*.
- Place in lightly greased baking pan.
- Brush each breast with olive oil, and sprinkle with salt and pepper.
- Bake for 40-45 minutes.

Serves 2-4

*Don't forget to remove toothpicks before serving!

Roasted Chicken

One 5 lb roasting chicken

Softened butter or canola oil

Salt and pepper

Optional *(for a richer flavor)*

Lemon slices

Celery leaves

Small onion, halved

- Preheat oven to 400°F.
- Remove any extra parts from inside the chicken.*
- Rinse chicken in cold water and dry with paper towel inside and out.
- Sprinkle inside of cavity with salt. *(Put lemon, celery leaves and onion half inside the cavity, if desired.)*
- Place in a roasting pan.
- Tie the legs together with a thread or cotton string.
- Brush the skin with canola oil or butter.
- Sprinkle with salt and pepper.
- Bake for approximately 2 hours. Check with a meat thermometer for doneness.

Serves 6-8

*FYI: Whole chickens and turkeys sometimes come with hearts, gizzards, etc. tucked inside the front and back cavities encased in plastic. Remember to remove when rinsing.

Encores:

Chicken Stir Fry

White Chicken Chili with Tomatoes *(see soups)*

Chicken Fajitas

Quick Chicken Divan

Encore: Chicken Stir Fry

1 tbsp sugar

1 tbsp soy sauce

1 tbsp sesame oil

1 tbsp butter

1 small onion, sliced thin

½ deli-roasted chicken or 2 cups cooked chicken

1½ cups snow peas

¼ - ½ cup cashew pieces

- Mix sugar and soy sauce in a small bowl until sugar is dissolved. Set aside.
- In a large wok or frying pan, melt the oil and butter.
- Cook the onion until lightly browned.
- Add chicken until heated through.
- Add snow peas, cashews, and soy sauce mixture.
- Cook quickly to warm thoroughly without overcooking the vegetables.

Serves 2

Encore: **Chicken Fajitas**

4 boneless, skinless chicken breasts sliced into strips*

1 large sweet onion, cut into ½" thick rings

1 red and 1 green pepper, sliced into strips

1 pkg of large flour tortillas

Marinade

¼ canola oil

2 tbsp lime juice

2 cloves garlic, chopped

2 tbsp soy sauce

½ tsp ground cumin

1 tsp celery salt

Toppings: salsa, shredded cheese, sour cream

- Combine marinade ingredients and mix well.
- Place chicken, peppers, and onions in a gallon-sized zippered bag and cover with marinade for at least 2 hours.
- When ready to cook, drain marinade.
- Using a greased skillet on a medium high heat, cook the chicken thoroughly and then add the vegetables. *(They will cook fast.)*
- Cover the tortillas with a damp paper towel and microwave for 1 minute to warm.
- Serve with desired toppings.

Serves 4-6

*Make a "Quick Chicken Fajita" by adding leftover chicken to sautéed onions and peppers. Place in warm tortillas and add toppings of choice.

Encore: **Quick Chicken Divan**

Spray oil

2 cups instant rice, cooked

2 cups of broccoli florets, cooked and drained

3 chicken breasts, cooked and torn into strips (can use deli-roasted chicken)

1 can cream of chicken soup

½ cup milk

1 cup grated sharp cheddar cheese

- Preheat oven to 350°F.
- Lightly grease a 9" x 13" baking dish.
- Spread cooked rice in the bottom of the baking dish, then add a layer of broccoli florets and top with the chicken.
- Mix soup and milk together and pour over the casserole. Top with cheddar cheese.
- Bake for 25 minutes.

Serves 2

Teriyaki Chicken
Bake or grill

4 boneless, skinless chicken breasts

One 13 oz can of pineapple rings, reserve juice

Teriyaki marinade*

- Place chicken breasts in a shallow dish or gallon zippered bag.
- Add pineapple juice to teriyaki marinade and pour over chicken.
- Marinate 8 hours or overnight.
- Preheat oven to 350°F.
- Remove chicken from marinade and place in roasting pan topped with pineapple rings. Cover pan with foil. *(If grilling, add pineapple for the last 5 minutes of cooking.)*
- Bake for 1 hour or grill over low heat.

Serves 2-4

*Teriyaki Marinade:
Good for chicken, pork, or beef

½ cup soy sauce

½ cup cooking sherry *(or water or white wine)*

1 tbsp garlic *(minced or powder)*

1 tbsp sugar

1 tbsp ground ginger

- Combine ingredients in bowl or jar and mix well.

FYI: Double marinade recipe for later use.

Penne Pasta with Shrimp and Artichoke Hearts

1 lb penne pasta, cooked according to package directions

2 tbsp garlic, minced

4 tbsp butter

2 tbsp olive oil

One 14.5 oz can diced tomatoes, undrained

Two 14 oz cans artichoke hearts, drained and quartered

½ cup fresh lemon juice

1 cup fresh basil, cut into strips*

1 lb shrimp, cooked and peeled

1½ cups feta cheese, crumbled

- In a large saucepan over medium heat, sauté garlic in butter and olive oil until light brown in color.
- Add tomatoes with juice, artichoke hearts, and lemon juice.
- Cover and reduce heat to low, simmering for 15 minutes.
- Add the cooked shrimp and basil to the tomato sauce and cover to heat through. *(Overcooking shrimp will make it tough.)*
- Remove from heat; toss with pasta and feta cheese.

Serves 4-6

*FYI: It's easiest to cut basil into strips if you roll each leaf from the tip to the stem end and slice into thin strips. This creates a basil chiffonade.

Shrimp Scampi over Linguine

4 tbsp butter

2 tbsp olive oil

2 lb large shrimp, peeled and de-veined

2 garlic cloves, minced

½ cup dry white wine

1 tbsp chopped parsley

2 tsp rosemary

¼ tsp salt *(or more to taste)*

¼ tsp pepper *(or more to taste)*

1 lb linguine, cooked according to package directions

1 cup freshly grated Parmesan cheese

- Heat butter and olive oil in a 12" frying pan over medium heat.
- Add a handful of shrimp at a time and sauté until just pink. Add garlic with the last handful of shrimp.
- Remove shrimp and garlic from pan, turn heat to medium high and add white wine. Quickly stir in parsley, rosemary, salt and pepper.
- Reduce heat to medium and stir in shrimp.
- Serve immediately over pasta and sprinkle with fresh Parmesan cheese.

Serves 6

Shrimp Foo Yong

1-2 cups shrimp, cooked and peeled

2 cups fresh bean sprouts, washed and drained

One 8 oz can of sliced water chestnuts, drained and sliced into strips

6 large eggs

¼ tsp ground ginger

1 tbsp soy sauce

4 green onions, sliced

2 tbsp cooking oil

- Mix all ingredients *(except the oil)* in a large mixing bowl.
- Heat 1 tbsp oil in a large skillet over medium-high heat
  (more oil may be added as needed).
- Dip and pour ¼ cup of the egg mixture for each individual foo yong, keeping them separated in the skillet like pancakes.
- When sides begin to brown, gently flip and cook other side.
- Drain on paper towels.

Serves 4

Boston Baked Scrod

1 lb cod filets

1½ cups milk

1 cup Ritz™ crackers, crushed

4 tbsp butter, cut into pats

- Preheat oven to 325°F.
- Cover fish with milk in an ungreased baking dish.
- Bake for 12 minutes.
- Pour off milk and top with cracker crumbs and butter.
- Broil for 3-4 minutes.

Serves 2

Baked Tilapia Filets

1 lb Tilapia filets

½ stick butter

½ tsp salt

½ tsp garlic powder

¼ cup Italian style breadcrumbs

¼ cup Parmesan cheese

- Preheat oven to 375°F.
- Mix dry ingredients in a shallow bowl. Set aside.
- Dip fillets in melted butter.
- Coat the fish with the breadcrumb mixture.
- Bake in a foil-lined pan lightly sprayed with cooking oil for 30 minutes or until fish flakes easily with a fork.

Serves 2

Bourbon Marinated Salmon

4 salmon filets *(approx. 6 oz each)*

½ cup brown sugar

1 jigger bourbon

½ cup soy sauce

- Whisk the brown sugar, bourbon, and soy sauce in a small bowl until the sugar is dissolved.
- Place the filets and marinade in a zippered gallon bag.
- Turn the bag to insure that the marinade completely covers all the filets. Refrigerate for 30 minutes to an hour.
- Pour off marinade.
- Place filets on a piece of foil and grill over medium heat for 20 minutes.

Serves 4

FYI: Fresh fish will not have a "fishy" smell. Fish should be cooked within 2 days of purchasing.

Pan Roasted Salmon
May also be grilled

4 salmon filets *(around 2¼-2½ lbs)*

2 tbsp olive oil, divided

2 tsp lemon pepper *(or lemon juice and black pepper)*

Salt and pepper to taste

- Preheat oven to 350°F.
- Line a baking pan with foil and drizzle with 1 tbsp of the olive oil.
- Lay the fish skin side down in the pan; drizzle with remaining 1 tbsp olive oil. Sprinkle with lemon pepper and salt.
- Bake for 40 minutes or until fish flakes easily with a fork.

Serves 4

Encore:

Wasabi Salmon Spread *(see Appetizers)*

Creamy Salmon Parmesan over Spinach Fettuccine

Scrambled Eggs and Salmon *(see Brunch)*

Encore: Creamy Salmon Parmesan over Spinach Fettuccine

2 cups cooked salmon

2 tbsp butter

2 cloves garlic, minced

2 tbsp flour

2 cups milk *(or 1 cup milk, 1 cup half-n-half)*

¾ cup grated Parmesan cheese

4 cups cooked spinach fettuccine

- Melt butter in a medium saucepan over medium heat.
- Add garlic and sauté quickly.
- Stir in flour.
- Slowly add milk, stirring constantly with a whisk. Cook until thickened.
- Add salmon and Parmesan. Cook until salmon is heated through.
- Spoon over hot fettuccine.

Serves 4

Pork Tenderloin in Ginger Sauce

Great served hot for fancy buffets or cold for picnics. All around hit!

1½-2 lb packaged pork tenderloin, rinsed, patted dry, and trimmed of fat.

Marinade

⅔ cup soy sauce

⅔ cup brown sugar

2 tbsp cornstarch

2 cloves garlic, minced

2 tbsp apple cider vinegar

2 tsp ground ginger

- Mix marinade ingredients together in a small bowl.
- Put tenderloins in a gallon-sized zipper bag and add marinade.
- Refrigerate overnight.
- Remove the meat from the marinade. Pour the marinade into a small saucepan; place the pork on a platter or in a roasting pan.
- Preheat the oven to 350°F OR heat the grill.
- Bring the marinade to a boil and then simmer for 5 minutes. Set aside.
- Cook the pork in the oven for 40-45 minutes or grill over medium heat for 25 minutes or until a thermometer reads 160°F.
- Serve hot with warm marinade or refrigerate pork and sauce to eat cold.

Serves 2-4

Pork Tenderloin in Citrus Juices with Mango Salsa *Delicious hot or cold*

One 1½ to 2 lb pkg. of pork tenderloin, rinsed, patted dry, and trimmed of fat

Marinade

1 cup orange juice

½ cup lime juice

1 tsp cumin

3 cloves garlic, minced

1 tsp crushed red pepper

½ tsp salt

- Place tenderloin in a gallon zippered bag.
- Combine remaining ingredients and pour over pork. Shake bag gently to evenly disperse marinade.
- Marinate 8 hours or overnight.
- Preheat oven to 325°F.
- Remove pork from marinade and place in shallow baking pan.
- Bake for 1 hour.
- Remove from oven and let sit for 10 minutes before slicing.
- Serve with mango salsa.*

Serves 4

*see Appetizers

Quick Grills

Grilled Chicken Breasts

4 skinless, boneless chicken breasts

1½ cups Kraft Italian Salad Dressing™

- Place chicken breasts in zippered plastic bag. Pour dressing over chicken and seal.
- Refrigerate for at least two hours.
- Remove chicken from marinade and grill over medium heat for 7 minutes per side.

Serves: 2

Corn on the Cob with Basil Butter is a great side with this.

Blackened Salmon Fillets

2 salmon fillets

Zatarain's Blackening Seasoning™ or other blackening seasoning

Olive oil

- Lightly brush fish with olive oil
- Rub top of fish with seasoning (seasoning is spicy, so sprinkle according to your taste)
- Grill on double layer of foil over medium heat for 15 minutes or until fish flakes easily with a fork.

Serves: 2

Consider Zucchini Skillet as a side dish.

Grilled Ribeyes

2 ribeye steaks

2 tsp. McCormick Montreal Steak Seasoning™ *

¼ cup olive oil

2 tbsp soy sauce

- Mix marinade ingredients in a small bowl.
- Pour over steaks and marinate for at least 30 minutes.
- Grill over medium heat until desired doneness, turning once half-way through *(approximately 8-12 minutes for medium rare and 12-15 for medium),*

Add Mandarin Orange Salad and Baked Potatoes for an easy company dinner.

*McCormick™ recipe from the label on seasoning bottle.

Pork Teriyaki Kabobs

One 1½ to 3 lb. pork tenderloin, rinsed, trimmed and cut into 1½" cubes

1 bottle teriyaki marinade

1 green pepper, cut into 1½" pieces

Cherry tomatoes

One 13½ oz can pineapple chunks, drained

1 medium red onion, quartered and separated

1 pkg wooden skewers *(grocery store purchase)*

- Place tenderloin cubes in plastic zippered gallon bag and cover with marinade.
- Refrigerate for at least 2 hours.
- Soak wooden skewers in water while meat is marinating *(this keeps the skewers from burning while on the grill).*
- Remove meat from marinade and alternate meat and vegetables on the skewers.
- Grill over medium heat approximately 5-8 minutes on each side.

Serves: 4-6

Serve over a flavored boxed rice (Pilaf, Saffron or Chicken)

Veggies and Sides

Vegetables and Sides

The high nutritional value of vegetables and sides makes this section an important part of your diet. These are some of the easiest dishes to prepare and many are readily microwaveable. You'll never turn your nose up at vegetables again once you have tried our recipes!

These tips will have you on your way to healthier and tastier meals.

Tips:

- Less is more. Overcooked vegetables lose color and nutritional value and may quickly become mushy and flavorless. To maintain maximum freshness, add a minimum amount of liquid to vegetables and quickly cook until tender-crisp using either the stovetop or microwave.

- Fresh is best. Buy seasonal produce for the best flavor and value. Handpick in small quantities as large bags are not economical for small households and often have mushy pieces.

- Frozen vegtables are convenient and economical. They are tastier and more nutritious than canned. Buy the unflavored varieties by the bag rather than by the box for a better value. Always keep an assortment in the freezer for quick additions to any meal.

- Frozen chopped onions, celery, and bell peppers are time savors.

- Frozen side dishes *(such as mac and cheese)* tend to be expensive, high in fat, sodium, and preservatives.

- Keep various rices, pastas, and grains in the pantry for quick side dishes.

- Canned goods can help in a hurry. A stock of low-sodium beans, petite diced tomatoes, and broths *(chicken, beef, and vegetable)* are good bases for soups, dips, sauces and a variety of side dishes.

Food in a Flash! Vegetables and Sides

Try these ideas for healthy and creative dishes.

Bagged Fresh Vegetables: Pre-cut, pre-washed* and ready to cook vegetables found bagged in the produce section are expensive, but a huge time saver. Added to fresh salads, used in stir-fry's, side dishes, or eaten raw, bagged vegetables are a great way to get your recommended dose of fresh veggies.

Frozen Vegetables: Steam, roast, or add to sauces *(such as spaghetti sauce)* for quick super sides! For an easy every-night side dish: put a small amount of any frozen vegetable in a bowl with a little water, cover with plastic wrap, and microwave for 4 minutes. Add salt and pepper to taste.

Frozen Sides: Scalloped Apples, Frozen Mashed Potatoes, Spinach Soufflé, Mac and Cheese are examples of the many sides available to add to a meat entrée for a quick meal, not the healthiest choice but good in a pinch.

Rice, Pasta, and Grains: Boxes of flavored rices, boil-in-bag rices, bagged noodle dishes, boxed couscous and quinoa are easy additions for a fast dinner.

* We recommend re-washing for safety.

Roasted Garlic Green Beans

1 lb fresh green beans or one 1 lb can of Blue Lake Italian green beans, drained

1 can roasted garlic flavored chicken broth

- Bring grean beans and broth to boil in a medium saucepan.
- Reduce heat and simmer to desired tenderness.

Serves 4

FYI: When green beans are cooked with a lid, they lose their bright green color.

Mrs. Mac's Baked Beans
A family picnic favorite

One 28 oz can original style baked beans

¼ cup onion, diced

¼ cup green pepper, diced

6 oz chili sauce *(found next to cocktail sauce and ketchup in grocery store)*

2 tbsp light brown sugar

1 strip bacon

- Preheat oven to 350°F.
- Mix all ingredients except bacon together in a large bowl.
- Pour into a large, deep casserole dish and top with bacon strip.
- Cover with foil.
- Cook covered for 15 minutes; uncover and cook for another 15 minutes.

Serves 6

Japanese Sesame Green Beans

1½ lbs slender green beans, washed and trimmed

1 tbsp sesame oil

1 tbsp butter

3 tsp sugar

1 tbsp soy sauce

1 tbsp roasted sesame seeds

- Dry green beans on a paper towel and set aside.
- Cook the butter, sesame oil, and sugar over medium heat until the sugar is melted.
- Quickly add in the green beans and soy sauce, stirring constantly and cooking to desired tenderness.
- Toss in sesame seeds and remove from heat.

Serves: 4

Baby Bok Choy
Good side for fish and chicken

4-6 baby bok choy *(Chinese cabbage, found in produce aisle)*

¼ cup soy sauce

1 tbsp sugar

1 tbsp butter

- Melt the butter in a 12" frying pan over low heat.
- Add soy sauce and sugar and stir until sugar is dissolved.*
- Increase heat to medium high. Quickly stir-fry the bok choy until it softens slightly and turns dark brown.
- Remove the bok choy from the pan and pour the remaining sauce over it.

Serves 4-6

*Optional Add ½ teaspoon of crushed red pepper flakes to the soy sauce and sugar.

Retro Broccoli Casserole

One 16 oz package of frozen chopped broccoli

½ cup milk

One 10 ¾ oz can of mushroom soup

1 cup mayonnaise

1 cup cheddar cheese, shredded

2 cups crushed cheese crackers

- Preheat oven to 350 degrees.
- Microwave broccoli for 5 minutes, drain excess liquid.
- Mix all ingredients *(except for cheese crackers)* and pour into a lightly greased 9"x13" casserole dish.
- Top with cheese crackers and bake for 40 minutes, uncovered.

Serves 8-10.

Roasted Garlic Cauliflower

Two 1lb pkgs frozen chopped cauliflower, thawed and drained

4-5 cloves fresh garlic, minced

½ cup olive oil

½ cup grated Parmesan cheese

1 bunch fresh parsley, chopped

- Preheat oven to 425° F.
- Lightly toss the cauliflower, garlic, and olive oil in a 9"x13" casserole dish.
- Stir in the chopped parsley and Parmesan, and then broil until slightly browned.

Serves 4-6

Microwaved Corn on the Cob with Basil Butter

4 ears of corn on the cob, cleaned of husks and silks

2 tbsp butter *(or more if desired)*

2 tsp dried or fresh chopped basil

Salt and pepper to taste

- Place corn in a shallow, microwave-safe baking dish. Add ½ cup of water and cover with plastic wrap.
- Microwave on high for 7-10 minutes. Peel back wrap and pour off water.
- Add basil and butter to dish. Roll each ear to cover with butter and basil.
- Sprinkle with salt and pepper.

Serves 4

Corn Pudding

One 15 oz can creamed corn

1 cup milk

2 eggs

3 tbsp butter, melted

2 tbsp flour

1 tbsp sugar

1 tsp salt

- Preheat oven to 325°F.
- Pour corn into a large bowl and stir in flour, salt, and sugar.
- Beat eggs in a medium bowl and add in milk and butter.
- Combine egg mixture into corn mixture and stir well.
- Pour into greased casserole dish and bake for 35-45 minutes.

Serves 4

Holiday Dressing

One 6 oz pkg cornbread mix

One 8 oz pkg prepared cornbread stuffing mix *(such as Pepperidge Farm™)*

2 stalks celery, chopped

2 onions, diced

1 stick butter

1 tbsp sage

Salt and pepper to taste

One 10¾ oz can chicken broth

- Preheat oven to 350°F.
- Cook cornbread according to package directions. Set aside to cool.
- In a large mixing bowl, crumble and combine the corn bread and stuffing mix. Set aside.
- Using a skillet, melt the butter over a medium heat and sauté the onions and celery until translucent.
- Add sage and cook 1 minute longer.
- Pour over the cornbread and stuffing mix, adding salt and pepper to taste.
- Add enough chicken broth as needed to dressing to achieve the consistency of raw cookie dough. Dressing should be moist before baking.
- Put the dressing in a 9"x13" casserole dish, cover with foil and bake for 30 minutes. Remove foil and bake uncovered for an additional 20 minutes or until top is browned.

Serves 8-12

Turkey Gravy

¼ cup turkey pan drippings

¼ cup all-purpose flour

1 cup turkey broth

water

- Place cooked turkey on a platter to cool . Pour turkey pan drippings into a two cup measuring cup. Refrigerate until the fat and broth are separated in the cup. *(Obviously, the amount of broth you have depends on the size of the turkey).*

- Skim fat off the top; pour ¼ cup of the fat into a sauce pan.

- Whisk in ¼ cup all-purpose flour.

- Cook the flour and fat for at least two minutes, stirring constantly until brown and smooth.

- Add enough water to the drippings to make two cups liquid.

- Slowly pour liquid into the flour/fat mixture, stirring constantly.

- Cook until thickened.

- Add salt and pepper to taste.

Makes 2 cups

Mashed Potatoes

4 Russet or Yukon Gold potatoes *(about 2 pounds)*, peeled
and cut into 2" cubes

¾ cup milk

½ stick butter

Salt and pepper

- Put the potato cubes in a large saucepan and cover with water.
- Bring water to a boil; reduce heat and cook for 15 minutes. Check with fork to see if potatoes are tender.
- Drain the water from the pot.
- Heat the milk and butter in a microwave until butter is melted, about 1 minute.
- Mash the potatoes with a mixer, slowly adding the milk and butter.
- Beat until smooth and creamy. *(Adjust with more milk, butter, salt and pepper for personal preference.)*

Serves 8

Roasted Garlic Mashed Potatoes

6 large unpeeled red potatoes cut into 2" cubes

2 cloves garlic

1 tsp olive oil

½ cup milk

2 tbsp butter

Salt and pepper

- Preheat oven to 400° F.

- Barely cover cubed potatoes with water, bring water to boil, then reduce heat and simmer for 20 minutes.

- While potatoes are cooking, put the garlic and oil in a square packet made from folded aluminum foil and bake for 10 minutes. Remove garlic from peel and set aside.

- When potatoes are tender, drain.

- Using a mixer, whip garlic, milk, butter and potatoes until fluffy.

- Salt and pepper to taste.

Serves 6-8

Microwaved Baked Potatoes
Make It A Meal!

2 large Russet or Idaho potatoes

Topping options: butter, salt, pepper, grated cheese, cooked broccoli, chili, sour cream, chives, crumbled bacon

- Scrub potato skins and pierce each one several times with a fork.
- Microwave on high for 10-12 minutes.

Serves 2

FYI : For a crispy potato skin: roll the cooked potatoes in melted butter; roll in salt and place on a baking sheet. Bake in a preheated 400°F oven for an additional 10 minutes.

Oven-Baked Sweet Potatoes

4 large sweet potatoes

Butter

Salt and pepper

- Preheat oven to 375°F.

- Scrub potatoes well and cut off pointed ends.

- Bake on a sheet of foil for 1 hour.

Serves 4

Microwaved Sweet Potato
Quick, easy and good for you

2 large sweet potatoes

Butter

Salt and pepper

- Scrub potato skins well and cut off pointed ends.

- Pierce each potato several times with a fork.

- Microwave on high for 8-10 minutes or until they feel soft.

Serves 2

FYI: If cooking more than 2 of either type of potatoes, it's more efficient to bake them in a conventional oven.

Roasted Rosemary Red Potatoes

8 medium red potatoes, cut into cubes

2 tablespoons olive oil

Salt and pepper

1 tbsp fresh rosemary, chopped, stems removed

- Place potatoes in a 9"x13" baking pan.
- Drizzle with olive oil and sprinkle with salt, pepper, and rosemary.
- Bake at 375° for 45 minutes.

Serves 6

Optional: For Roasted Rosemary-Garlic Red Potatoes, sprinkle 2 tsp minced garlic on potatoes with the other seasonings.

Scalloped Gruyere Potatoes

No one would even guess they're not from scratch!

One 4 oz box scalloped potatoes

2 cups boiling water

⅔ cup milk

1 tbsp butter

Cheese packet

½ cup Gruyere cheese, grated

1 tsp fresh rosemary, chopped (optional)

- Preheat oven to 375°F.
- Prepare potatoes according to package directions; top with Gruyere cheese and sprinkle with rosemary.
- Bake as directed on box.

Serves 4-6

Basic White Rice

For the rice purist

2 cups long grain white rice, washed

2 cups cold water

- Wash rice thoroughly.
- In a medium saucepan, combine the rice and water.
- Bring to a boil with the pan uncovered.
- When the water begins to boil rapidly, reduce the heat to low and cover the pan.
- Cook for 20 minutes.
- Do not remove the lid or steam pressure will be lost.

Serves 4

FYI: How to wash rice: Raw rice is often not clean, so it is necessary to wash it before cooking. Put the rice in a saucepan and cover with water. Stir the rice with a spoon or your fingers. Pour out the water. Repeat the process at least 3 times, then proceed with cooking.

FYI: "Dirty" rice water is good to water plants as it has minerals and nutrients in it.

Consommé Rice

2 tbsp butter

½ cup onion, chopped

One 10½ oz can consommé soup

2 cups instant rice

Salt and pepper

- Melt butter in a 12″ skillet over medium heat.
- Add onions and sauté until tender.
- Stir in rice, then soup, salt and pepper.
- Cover and simmer for 15 minutes or until soup is absorbed and rice is fluffy.

Serves 4-6

Fast Fried Rice

One 10 oz pkg frozen green peas

6 slices bacon

4 green onions, chopped

4 cups cooked white rice

2 tbsp soy sauce

Salt to taste

- Prepare peas according to package directions and set aside.
- Fry the bacon on a medium heat until crisp then remove from the skillet leaving the bacon drippings in the pan.
- Crumble the bacon and set aside.
- Sauté the green onions in the bacon drippings, then add the rice and cook for 3 minutes over medium heat.
- Gently stir in the bacon, peas and soy sauce.
- Salt to taste.

Serves 6-8

Optional: Scramble 2 eggs after cooking the bacon, remove from skillet and add back in with the bacon, peas, and soy sauce.

Spinach with Pine Nuts and Apples

2 tbsp olive oil

One 3 oz pkg of pine nuts

3 cloves garlic, chopped

1 Granny Smith apple, unpeeled and diced

Two 6 oz pkgs of fresh spinach

Salt to taste

- Sauté pine nuts and garlic in olive oil until lightly browned.
- Quickly add in apple and cook until slightly tender.
- Add spinach by handfuls until all is wilted.
- Salt to taste.

Serves 4

Maggie's Spinach Pie

One 10 oz pkg frozen, chopped spinach

One 3 oz pkg cream cheese, softened

1 cup sharp cheddar cheese, shredded

5 eggs, slightly beaten

½ tsp salt

¼ cup green onion, chopped

2 tbsp parsley, chopped

One 9" unbaked pie crust

1 tomato, thinly sliced and drained on a paper towel

¼ cup Parmesan cheese

- Preheat oven to 400°F.
- Microwave spinach for 3-5 minutes on high, drain well and squeeze out remaining water.
- Combine cream cheese, cheddar cheese, eggs, salt, onions, and parsley and beat lightly with a fork.
- Stir in spinach and pour into pie crust.
- Arrange tomato slices on top and sprinkle with Parmesan cheese.
- Bake for 30 minutes or until set.

Serves 6-8

Spanakopeta

One 8 oz pkg phyllo dough, thawed*

1 lb feta cheese, crumbled

8 eggs

3 bunches green onions, chopped

2 lbs of frozen spinach, thawed and squeezed dry

1½ sticks of butter, melted

- Preheat oven to 375°F.
- In large mixing bowl, combine eggs, feta cheese, onions, and spinach. Set aside.
- Butter the bottom and sides of a 9"x13" pan.
- Place 8-10 sheets of phyllo on the bottom, brushing each sheet with melted butter.
- Spread ½ of the spinach mixture on top.
- Top with 2 more sheets of phyllo, brushing each sheet with butter.
- Repeat this process 2 more times.
- Cover with 8-10 sheets of phyllo, buttering each sheet as you layer.
- Before baking, use a sharp knife and cut the spanakopeta in lengthwise rows of desired width.
- Bake for 30 minutes.
- Reduce the heat to 350°F and bake an additional 45 minutes.
- Cool slightly before cutting crosswise to make individual squares.
- May be frozen for later use.

Serves 8-12

Cover thawed phyllo dough with a damp paper towel to keep pliable.

Zucchini Sesame Stir-fry

7 oz *(or ½ cake)* of firm or extra firm tofu, cut into ½"squares*

1 medium zucchini, sliced into thin strips

1 onion, sliced into strips

2 cups fresh bean sprouts

1 tbsp sugar

1 tbsp soy sauce

1 tbsp butter

1 tbsp sesame oil

- Place all washed and prepared vegetables on a platter and set aside.
- Mix the sugar and soy sauce in a small bowl until the sugar is dissolved and set aside.
- In a large wok or frying pan, melt the butter and sesame oil together over medium to high heat.
- Cook the onion slightly, add the zucchini and then add the tofu and sprouts.
- Pour the sugar/soy sauce mixture over the top and stir gently.
- Quickly remove from heat and serve.

Serves 4

FYI:

1. This process goes very fast! Be sure to have all ingredients ready to go.

2. Cooked chicken and shrimp are delicious additions to this recipe.

*Optional but good source of protein.

Zucchini Skillet

Yummy summer side dish

2 small zucchini, cut into ¼" rounds

2 tbsp butter

½ small onion, cut into thin slices

1 teaspoon oregano

1 cup corn kernels, fresh or frozen

1 large tomato, cut into wedges

Salt and pepper to taste

- Melt butter over medium heat in a 12" skillet.
- Layer zucchini and onion in butter and sprinkle with oregano. Cover the pan.
- Cook over low heat for 5 minutes until zucchini and onions soften.
- Remove cover and stir in the corn, tomato, and salt and pepper to taste.
- Cook over low heat for 5 minutes.

Serves 4

Bread

Breads

There's nothing better than the aroma of freshly baked bread wafting through your home unless it's the ease of picking up great ready-made bread from the bakery or grocery store. Here are some suggestions to ensure that you will have delicious bread ready when you are.

Tips:

- While a very admirable and tasty endeavor, bread making does tend to be time consuming. We say – save bread making for a rainy day activity, double the recipes and fill your freezer!

- On busy days, try the many wonderful types of bread available in bakeries, delis, and the frozen food section of the grocery store. They are relatively inexpensive and save your precious time.

Food in a Flash! Bread

Keep these items in your freezer and pantry for that "homemade" aroma and taste without the fuss:

Frozen biscuits

Frozen yeast rolls

Frozen loaves of bread

Boxed bread mixes

Boxed cornbread mixes

Boxed biscuit mix

Strawberry Nut Bread
Yummy and pretty holiday treat

Two 10 oz pkgs frozen, sliced strawberries in syrup

3 cups all-purpose flour

1 tbsp cinnamon

1 tsp baking soda

1 tsp salt

4 eggs

1 cup vegetable oil

1 cups sugar

1¼ cup chopped pecans or walnuts

- Preheat oven to 350°F.
- Grease two 5½" x 9½"loaf pans.
- Defrost strawberries.
- Mix together the flour, cinnamon, baking soda, and salt in a medium bowl.
- In a large mixing bowl, beat eggs until fluffy. Then beat in oil, sugar, and strawberries with syrup.
- Gradually add flour mixture to egg/strawberry mixture and mix well.
- Stir in nuts.
- Pour half of the mixture into each pan.
- Bake for 1 hour and 10 minutes.

Yields 2 loaves

Pumpkin Bread

3⅓ cups flour

½ tsp baking powder

2 tsp baking soda

1½ tsp salt

1 tsp cinnamon

1 tsp ground cloves

2⅓ cups sugar

⅔ cup Crisco shortening

4 eggs

One 15 oz can pumpkin

⅔ cup water

⅓ cup nuts *(pecans or black walnuts)*

⅓ cup golden or regular raisins

- Preheat oven to 350°F.
- Grease two 5½" x 9½" loaf pans.
- Sift together flour, baking powder, baking soda, salt, cinnamon, and cloves. Set aside.
- In a separate mixing bowl, cream sugar and shortening.
- Add eggs, pumpkin, and water.
- Gradually add flour mixture to pumpkin mixture. Mix well.
- Stir in nuts and raisins.
- Pour into loaf pans.
- Bake for 1 hour.

Yields 2 loaves

Sour Cream Coffee Swirl

Cake

1 box yellow cake mix with pudding

4 eggs

1 cup sour cream

½ cup canola oil

Topping

1 cup pecans, chopped

½ cup brown sugar

1 tbsp cinnamon

- Preheat oven to 325°F.
- Grease a tube or bundt pan.*
- Mix cake ingredients in a large bowl on medium speed for 2 minutes.
- In a separate smaller bowl, mix topping ingredients together with a spoon.
- Spoon 1/3 of the topping mixture into the bottom of the greased pan.
- Pour half of the batter over the topping mixture.
- Spoon the remainder of the topping mixture over the batter. Swirl the sugar/cinnamon gently into the batter.
- Add the remainder of the batter.
- Bake 40-45 minutes for bundt or tube pan; 25-30 minutes for cake pans.

Serves 8-10

*FYI: If bundt or tube pans are not available, use 2 greased cake pans. Pour batter in pans. Swirl a small amount of topping into batter and top with remaining topping.

Parmesan Cheese Toasts

Nice accompaniment to soups or salads

1 stick salted butter, melted

1 cup corn flakes, finely crushed

1 cup Parmesan cheese, finely grated

1 loaf Pepperidge Farm™ thinly sliced white bread

- Preheat oven to 375°F.

- In a shallow glass plate, melt the butter in the microwave on low heat. Cover with paper towel or napkin to prevent splatters.

- In another shallow dish, combine cornflakes and Parmesan cheese.

- Remove crust from bread and slice into strips 1" wide.

- Dip bread strips into butter, then into bread crumbs, coating on both sides.

- Place on baking sheet and bake for 8 minutes or until golden brown.

Parmesan Cheese Crisps

Freshly grated Parmesan cheese

Spray oil

- Preheat oven to 450°F.
- Spray a large cookie sheet with oil.
- Drop 1 tbsp of freshly grated Parmesan cheese on the cookie sheet.
- Using the back of a spoon, spread the cheese flat.
- Make as many as you need. *You'll want to make a lot!*
- Bake for 5-6 minutes.
- Let cool and carefully remove with a spatula.
- Good with soups and salads.

FYI: These are delicate – handle with care!

Melt in Your Mouth Muffins

Spray oil

1 stick butter, softened

One 8 oz pkg cream cheese, softened

1 cup self-rising flour

- Preheat oven to 400°F.
- Spray 2 miniature muffin tins with oil.
- In medium bowl, beat butter and cream cheese until creamy.
- Slowly add small amounts of flour until blended.
- Fill muffin tins with dough.
- Bake for 15 minutes.
- Best served immediately. Can be reheated in the microwave. *(Takes 10 seconds.)*

Yields 18 mini muffins

Cheesy Cornbread Muffins

2 cups self-rising cornmeal

½ tsp salt

3 eggs

1 cup cottage cheese

1 cup extra sharp cheddar cheese

½ cup buttermilk

½ cup canola oil

½ cup sour cream

1 tsp sugar

- Preheat oven to 350°F.
- Combine all ingredients in a large mixing bowl.
- Spoon into a lightly greased muffin tin.
- Bake for 30-35 minutes or until lightly browned.

Yields 1½ - 2 dozen medium muffins

Biscotti

Great gift idea!

2 sticks butter, softened

1 cup sugar

4 eggs

1 tsp vanilla

4 slight cups flour

1 tsp baking soda

1 tsp baking powder

1 tbsp black pepper

3 cups almonds *(or other nuts such as pecans)*

- Beat butter, sugar, eggs, and vanilla in a large mixing bowl.
- Mix flour, soda, baking soda, baking powder, and pepper in a separate bowl.
- Using your hands, slowly add the flour mixture to the egg mixture and work in nuts.
- Make 6 balls and place on 2 cookie sheets. Refrigerate overnight.
- NEXT DAY: Preheat oven to 325°F.
- Knead the biscotti balls on a floured surface, forming 6 loaves.
- Place 3 loaves on 1 cookie sheet for a total of 2 cookie sheets.
- Bake for 30 minutes or until tops are lightly browned.
- Cool slightly and cut into ½"- ¾"slices. Return to cookie sheet standing each biscotti upright and not touching.
- Reduce heat to 250°F and bake until crisp, approximately 1 hour.

Yields 48 biscotti

Quick Foccaccia

Spray oil

1 loaf of frozen bread dough

Olive oil

Garlic salt

1½ tsp rosemary

1 tbsp Parmesan cheese

- Spray a 10" x 15" baking sheet with oil. Place loaf of frozen dough on sheet and allow it to thaw at room temperature.

- Preheat oven to 375°F.

- When thawed, press dough flat into a rectangle. Make indentations over entire top with thumb about 5" apart.

- Brush with olive oil; sprinkle with garlic salt, rosemary, and Parmesan cheese.

- Bake for 25 minutes.

Serves 8

Desserts

Dessert

The Grande Finale! Make it delectably light or serioulsy rich. Follow these tips and have a delicious ending to your meal.

Tips:

- Match the meal- light meals *(such as salad)* can accommodate a heavier dessert while heavier meals encourage a lighter dessert.

- Make desserts ahead of time to ease meal preparation.

- For added fun, match the dessert to the entrée "theme." *(i.e. serve Mango Ginger Ice Cream with an Asian inspired meal).*

Food in a Flash! **Desserts**

Mouthwatering desserts are readily available in bakeries, delis, and restaurants. A great trick when time is running short! Try these:

- Angel food cake with various toppings *(berries, whipped cream, chocolate sauce)*
- Sherbet or sorbet with lemon thins or gingersnaps
- Fruit and cheese *(e.g. Raclette and red grapes)*
- Ice cream and toppings with a lemon thin cookie
- Frozen pies and cakes
- Frozen cheesecakes
- Frozen mini cream puffs and éclairs
- Frozen cobblers
- Bakery brownies
- Various fruits dipped in melted chocolate

Strawberry Shortcake

Traditional springtime recipe but good any time of year!

1 quart of strawberries, sliced

2½ cups biscuit mix

½ cup buttermilk

6 tbsp sugar, divided

Whipped cream to taste

4 tbsp butter, melted

6 whole strawberries for garnish

- Preheat oven to 425°F.
- Add 3 tbsp of the sugar to the sliced strawberries and gently toss. Set aside.
- Combine the baking mix, buttermilk, remaining 3 tbsp of sugar, and melted butter. Stir until a soft dough forms.
- Drop 6 large spoonfuls onto an ungreased baking sheet forming 6 shortcakes.
- Bake for 20 minutes or until the tops of the short cakes are golden in color.
- Cool slightly and then cut each shortcake in half.
- Spoon the strawberries, along with some of the reserved juices, onto the bottom half of the shortcake.
- Add the other half and top with the desired amount of whipped cream.
- Garnish with a whole strawberry.

Serves 6

FYI: Make the shortcakes ahead of time and then add the fruit and whipping cream before serving!

Variations Use fresh peaches or raspberries *(frozen will do)*.

Fruit Trifle

1 prepared angel food cake or pound cake cut into 1 inch pieces

4 cups fresh sliced fruit (strawberries, peaches, kiwis, blueberries, etc.)

2 pkgs instant vanilla pudding, prepared according to package directions

1 container whipped topping

- In a clear glass bowl, alternate layers of cake, fruit, then pudding.
- Top with whipped cream.
- Refrigerate until ready to serve.

Serves 8-10

Variations Make individual servings in wine glasses or goblets. A little rum may be added to the pudding for an extra "kick". For a chocolate trifle: substitute brownies for cake and use chocolate pudding.

Fruit Stuffed Pineapple with Lemon Cream Dip *Delicious and looks great on a buffet table*

1 ripe pineapple

3 cups of cubed or sliced fruit
(peaches, strawberries, grapes, cantaloupe- whatever is in season)

Lemon Dip

1 small container of whipped topping

1 jar of lemon curd or 2 cups of lemon flavored pudding snack

- Place the pineapple on a cutting board and slice in half *(start at the base of the pineapple and cut all the way through the stem)*.

- Cut the pineapple out by chunks *(discard the hard core going down the center)* taking care not to pierce the pineapple's skin.

- Place chunks of pineapple in a bowl. Set aside.

- Turn each pineapple shell over on a paper towel to drain until ready to fill.

- When ready to serve, place pineapple halves side by side on a platter with the stems pointing in opposite directions.

- Gently toss the pineapple chunks with the other fruit and mound into each half.

- In a medium bowl, fold the lemon curd or pudding into the whipped cream until blended. Spoon the cream into a smaller glass bowl. Put toothpicks in a shot glass near the fruit for dipping or place a small serving spoon in the cream.

Serves a crowd

Quick Key Lime Pie

One 14 oz can sweetened condensed milk

½ cup key lime or freshly squeezed lime juice

1 pre-made graham cracker crust

Whipped topping

- Mix condensed milk and lime juice. Pour into pie shell.
- Cover and refrigerate for at least 4 hours.
- Top with whipped topping.

Serves 6-8

Key Lime Meringue Pie

1 pre-made graham cracker crust

4 eggs, separated in this manner: 4 yolks in one bowl; 3 whites in a second bowl; 1 white in a third bowl.*

One 14 oz can sweetened condensed milk

½ cup key lime juice

¼ tsp cream of tartar

6 tbsp sugar

1 tsp vanilla

- Preheat oven to 375°F.
- In a small bowl, beat one egg white until stiff. Set aside.
- In a medium bowl, beat the egg yolks and condensed milk until blended.
- Slowly add lime juice to condensed milk/egg yolk mixture.
- Gently fold in the single beaten egg white.
- Pour into graham cracker crust.
- In another medium bowl, beat 3 remaining egg whites and the cream of tarter until foamy. Add sugar, 1 tbsp at a time until stiff peaks form (could take about 5 minutes). Add vanilla and mix well.
- Spread meringue over the top of warm pie filling, covering the crust as meringue shrinks inward while baking.
- Bake for 5-10 minutes, checking constantly to see that top lightly browns but doesn't burn.
- Cool; cover and refrigerate for at least 4 hours.

Serves 6-8

*FYI: For fluffy meringue, make sure there are no yolks in the egg whites and that bowls and beaters are clean and dry.

Fruit Pizza

3 cups of assorted seasonal fruit, sliced if necessary
(strawberries, nectarines, kiwis, blueberries)

Dough

1½ cups flour

¾ cup confectioner's sugar

1 stick butter, melted

Filling

One 8 oz pkg. cream cheese, softened

½ cup sour cream

½ cup sugar

½ tsp vanilla

Glaze

½ cup sugar

2 tbsp cornstarch

½ cup orange juice

½ cup water

1 tsp lemon juice

- Preheat oven to 375°F.

- Mix dough ingredients and press into the bottom of a 12" pizza pan, forming a slight rim around the edge. Prick entire surface with a fork, to avoid an uneven crust.

- Bake for 8-10 minutes until crust is lightly browned. Cool.

- Mix the filling ingredients and spread on top of the cooled crust.

- Decorate this entire layer with fruit *(e.g. an outer row of nectarine slices, two rows of strawberry slices, a row of kiwi slices, and blueberries in the center).*

- Cook the glaze ingredients in a small saucepan, stirring constantly until it comes to a boil. Let glaze cool for 5 minutes.

- Spoon the glaze over the entire pizza. Refrigerate uncovered for 30 minutes then cover with waxed paper until serving time.

Serves 2

Lemon Ice Box Pie

That delicious pie your grandmother makes!

One 8 oz container of whipped topping

One 14 oz can sweetened condensed milk

1 small can frozen lemonade

1 pre-made graham cracker crust

Canned whipped cream

1 fresh lemon, thinly sliced

- Using a mixer, blend the whipped topping, condensed milk, and lemonade together in a large bowl.
- Pour into the crust, cover and freeze.
- Decorate with the canned whipped cream and thin lemon twists.*

Serves 6

*FYI: How to make a LEMON TWIST: Slice a 1/8" round of lemon, and then cut the slice in half. Cut the half down the center, gently twist and place on top of the whipped cream!

Easy Chocolate Pie

¼ cup cocoa

¼ cup plain flour

1 cup sugar

1 stick butter, melted

¼ tsp vanilla

2 eggs

One 8" unbaked pie shell *(not deep dish)*

- Preheat oven to 350°F.
- Mix the cocoa, flour, and sugar together.
- Stir in the butter, vanilla, and eggs.
- Pour into the unbaked pie shell and bake for 35 minutes.
- Serve with vanilla ice cream or whipped cream.

Serves 6-8

Ice Cream Sundae Pie

No cooking involved

1 pre-made chocolate cookie pie crust

1 half gallon vanilla ice cream *(or flavor of choice)*

1 jar chocolate fudge sauce

1 can whipped cream

Cherries

½ cup peanuts, chopped *(optional)*

- Soften ice cream by leaving it at room temperature for 8-15 minutes.
- With a large spoon, spread softened ice cream over bottom of the cookie crust.
- Cover with plastic wrap *(or the plastic top that came with the crust)* and freeze for 1 hour.
- Remove from freezer and pour enough chocolate sauce to cover the ice cream. Re-cover and refreeze.
- Remove from freezer 10 minutes before serving. When soft enough to cut, slice into 6 servings.
- Top with whipped cream, nuts, and a cherry.

Serves 6

Mango-Ginger Ice Cream

One ½ gal vanilla ice cream, softened

2 cups fresh mango slices *(or use the fresh "jarred" mango found in the produce section, drained)*

2 tsp ground ginger *(more if you prefer a "bite")*

- Chop the mango either by hand or with a blender into ¼" pieces.
- Stir the chopped mango and ginger into the softened ice cream.
- Refreeze.
- Garnish with fresh mint sprigs, if desired.

Serves 6-8

FYI: Ginger is spicy so add with caution!

Mud Slide Shakes

4 cups coffee ice cream

1 tbsp chocolate syrup

2 cups milk

Kahlua™ liquor to taste

Whipped cream

- Blend the first 4 ingredients together, adding the milk a little at a time, until smooth.
- Pour into tall frosted glasses and top with whipping cream.
- YUM!

Serves 2

Peanut Butter Shakes

4 cups chocolate ice cream

2 tbsp smooth peanut butter

2 cups milk

Whipped cream

- Blend the first 3 ingredients together, adding the milk a little at a time, until smooth.
- Pour into tall frosted glasses and top with whipping cream.
- YUM!

Serves 2

Amaretto Cheesecake

Crust

40 vanilla wafers *(about 1 box)*, crushed

¾ cup slivered almonds, toasted and chopped*

⅓ cup sugar

¼ cup plus 1 tbsp melted butter

- Combine the above ingredients in a mixing bowl and mix thoroughly.
- Press evenly into the bottom and sides of a spring-form pan. Set aside.

* To toast almonds: Spread in an even layer on the bottom of an ungreased skillet and stir over medium-high heat until browned. Remove and cool on paper towels.

Filling

Three 8 oz pkgs of cream cheese, softened

1 cup sugar

4 eggs

⅓ cup whipping cream

¼ cup amaretto liqueur

1 tsp vanilla

- Preheat the oven to 350°F.
- Mix the above ingredients and pour into the crust.
- Bake for 20 minutes, then reduce the heat to 250°F and bake for 1 hour 15 minutes. *(Mixture will be creamy and loose.)*
- Cool for 15 minutes, then refrigerate overnight to set.
- May be frozen.

Serves 6-8

FYI: Well worth the effort!

Apple Crumble
The Ultimate Cold Weather Comfort Food

4 large Granny Smith apples, sliced into thin wedges

1 cup sugar, divided

1 tsp cinnamon

¾ cup flour

⅓ cup butter

Vanilla ice cream *(optional)*

- Preheat oven to 400°F.
- Heap the apples into a 2 quart casserole dish.
- Sprinkle ½ cup of the sugar and the cinnamon over the apples.
- In a small bowl, blend the remaining ½ cup sugar, flour, and butter with a fork until the mixture is crumbly.
- Heap the flour mixture over the apples.
- Bake for 10 minutes. Reduce the heat to 350°F and bake an additional 30 minutes or until the apples are tender.
- Best served warm with a scoop of vanilla ice cream!

Serves 4-6

Peach Crisp

6-8 peaches, peeled and sliced

½ cup brown sugar

¾ cup flour

½ cup butter

½ tsp cinnamon

- Preheat oven to 350°F.
- Butter glass pie pan and add peaches.
- Blend sugar, flour, butter, and cinnamon with a fork until crumbly.
- Sprinkle over peaches.
- Bake for 30 minutes.

Serves 4-6

Almond Torte

Makes a delicious gift

1½ sticks butter, softened

1½ cups sugar

2 eggs

1½ cups all purpose flour

Pinch of salt

1 tsp almond extract

⅓ cup slivered almonds

1½ tbsp sugar *(for topping)*

- Preheat oven to 350°F.
- Line a 9" glass pie plate with foil.
- Combine butter and sugar in a mixing bowl.
- Add eggs, one at a time, beating after each addition.
- Add flour, salt, almond extract and beat well.
- Spread mixture into pie plate, sprinkle with almonds and 1 tbsp sugar.
- Bake for 30-40 minutes or until golden brown.
- Let cool 1 hour, then carefully slide the cake off the foil onto a serving dish.

Serves 6-8

Pecan Pie

1 unbaked 9" deep-dish pie shell

3 large eggs

1 cup light corn syrup

1 cup sugar

2 tbsp butter, melted

1 tsp vanilla

1½ cups pecans *(halves or pieces)*

- Preheat oven to 350°F.
- Lightly beat eggs in a medium-sized bowl.
- Add corn syrup, sugar, margarine, and vanilla.
- Stir in pecans.
- Pour into pie shell and place on a baking sheet.
- Cover edges of crust with strips of aluminum foil to prevent over-browning.
- Bake for 45-50 minutes or until center of pie seems firm.

Serves 8

Pumpkin Pie

One 9" deep dish pie shell, baked according to pkg directions

2 cups canned pumpkin

1 cup whipped cream

½ cup brown sugar, firmly packed

2 eggs

½ tsp ginger

1 tsp cinnamon

½ tsp cloves

Canned whipped cream or topping for garnish

- Preheat oven to 375°F.
- Beat pumpkin, cream, eggs, sugar, and spices with a mixer.
- Pour into baked pie shell.
- Cover edges of crust with foil.
- Bake for 40 minutes or until center seems to be set.

Serves 8

Swedish Brownies

2 sticks butter, melted

3 tbsp cocoa powder

2 cups sugar

4 eggs

1½ cups flour

2 tsp vanilla

½ cup chopped nuts *(pecans or walnuts)*

- Preheat oven to 350°F.
- Combine the first six ingredients in a large bowl. When well mixed, add nuts.
- Spread in a greased 9"x13" pan and bake for 20 minutes.

Serves 10-12

Super Easy Chocolate Chip Brownies

2 rolls chocolate chip cookie dough

Two 8 oz pkgs cream cheese

1½ cups sugar

3 eggs

- Preheat oven to 375°F.
- Press 1 roll of cookie dough in the bottom of a 9"x13" baking dish.
- Mix the cream cheese, sugar, and eggs together in a mixing bowl. Spread over the cookie dough layer.
- Drop spoonfuls of the remaining roll of cookie dough over the cream cheese layer.
- Bake for 40 minutes.

Serves 10-12

Shortcut Chocolate Chip Cookies

1 pkg yellow cake mix

2 eggs

½ cup vegetable oil

1 cup semi-sweet chocolate chips

- Preheat oven to 350°F.
- In a large bowl, combine cake mix, oil, and eggs with a wooden spoon.
- Stir in chocolate chips.
- Drop by tablespoons onto a cookie sheet.
- Bake for 9-11 minutes.

Makes 1½ dozen

Cut and Bake Peanut Butter Cup Cookies

1 roll of slice-and-bake prepared sugar cookie dough

36 miniature peanut butter cup candies

- Preheat oven to 375°F.
- Cut cookie dough into 9 equal slices and then cut each slice into quarters.
- Place one piece in each cup of a greased miniature muffin tin.
- Bake for 10 minutes.
- Unwrap the candies while the cookies are baking.
- Place one piece of candy into each cup upon removing from oven.
- Cool for 10 minutes, then carefully remove from pan and cool further on paper towels.

Makes 36 cookies

Chinese Almond Cookies

2 cups butter, softened

1½ cups sugar

1 tsp almond extract

4 cups all-purpose flour

¼ tsp salt

1 cup whole almonds

- In a large mixing bowl, cream the butter, sugar, and almond extract.
- Slowly mix in flour and salt.
- Blend thoroughly.
- Cover and refrigerate at least 3 hours.
- Preheat oven to 300°F.
- Drop the dough by teaspoonfuls onto a cookie sheet and press flat.
- Press a whole almond on top of each cookie.
- Bake for 30 minutes.

Makes 2 dozen

Serve with mango-ginger ice cream.

Angel Food Sherbet Cake

1 ready-made Angel Food Cake

1 quart raspberry sherbet

1 quart lemon *(or lime)* sherbet

1 large container strawberry *(or plain)* whipped topping

- Leave raspberry sherbet at room temperature for about 8 minutes to soften slightly.
- Slice angel food cake into 3 layers with serrated knife. Place bottom layer on a freezer-safe plate.
- Spread raspberry sherbet in a neat 1" layer over bottom layer of Angel Food Cake.
- Place middle layer of Angel Food Cake over raspberry sherbet. Cover all with plastic wrap and place in the freezer for at least an hour.
- Let lemon sherbet soften at room temperature for about 8 minutes.
- Remove cake from freezer and spread neatly with 1" layer of lemon sherbet.
- Place top layer of cake over lemon sherbet; cover with plastic wrap and freeze again for at least an hour.
- When ready to serve, frost entire cake with whipped topping.
- Cut* and serve.
- If there is cake left over, re-cover with plastic and re-freeze.

Serves 8-10

* For easy slicing: dip long serated knife in a glass of warm water, wipe then cut. The warm knife makes slicing frozen ice cream much easier.

Eunice's Easy Peanut Butter Fudge

One 12 oz pkg semi-sweet chocolate morsels

One 12 oz jar of creamy peanut butter

One 14 oz can sweetened condensed milk

- Cook the chocolate chips and peanut butter together in a microwave for 3 minutes or until melted.
- Stir well; add condensed milk. Blend thoroughly.
- Spread on a waxed-paper lined 8"x8" pan.
- Chill until hard.
- Cut into squares.

Makes 2 dozen

Chocolate Dipped Strawberries

1 lb whole strawberries with stem intact, washed and patted dry with paper towel.

12 oz semi-sweet chocolate chops

- Place chocolate chips in a microwave-safe bowl.

- It's easy to burn the chocolate in the microwave, so proceed cautiously: Melt chocolate for 1 minute on medium power. Stir. Return and heat on medium power for 30 seconds. Stir again.

- Hold the strawberry by the stem and dip into the warm chocolate, letting the excess chocolate drip into the bowl.

- Place the strawberry onto a piece of wax paper and let set until firm *(around 30 minutes)*.

Serves 6-8

Brunch

Brunch

The wonderful combination of late breakfast and early lunch, brunch is one of the easiest ways to entertain friends. Check out our tips and discover what fun midmorning parties can be!

Tip:

- A brunch menu usually includes an egg dish or casserole, potatoes, or bread, fruit and maybe meat *(i.e. Mexican Brunch Casserole, coffee cake, sausage patties, and sliced melon.)*

- Keep it simple. Select easy prep recipes and dishes that can be prepared ahead.

- Set the table the night before.

- Buffets help make morning entertainment easier for the hostess.

- Brunches are great for bridal showers, holiday gatherings, and for entertaining overnight guests. Consider setting up outside in the spring or inside in the winter next to a cozy fire.

Food in a Flash! **Brunch**

Relax! Keep these low prep items on hand for a stress free brunch that you and your guests will enjoy!

Eggs

Grated cheeses

Cream cheese *(for dips and spreads)*

Orange juice

Fresh fruit

Canned fruits *(for cooking and easy fruit salads)*

A variety of breads and rolls
(keep some in the freezer: bagels, English muffins, muffins, coffee cakes)

Smoked salmon

Frozen quiche *(regular or minis)*

Frozen hash browns

Frozen sausage patties

Baked Fruit
Good for brunch or with ham or pork

One 8 oz can pineapple chunks

One 29 oz can pear slices

One 29 oz can peach slices

One 16 oz can apricot halves

One 16 oz can plums

½ cup butter

¾ cup light brown sugar

1 tbsp corn starch

- Preheat oven to 350°F.
- Butter glass 9" x 13" casserole dish.
- Drain juice from all fruit, reserving 1 cup.
- Arrange fruit in casserole dish.
- Melt butter over low heat in a medium saucepan. Stir in brown sugar and cornstarch. Slowly add juice.
- Bring to a boil, stirring constantly. Let simmer for 5 minutes.
- Pour over fruit.
- Bake for 40-45 minutes or until liquid bubbles in center.

Serves 10

Mexican Brunch Casserole

Can assemble and refrigerate the night before

10 eggs

½ cup flour

One 12 oz carton cottage cheese

8 oz Monterrey Jack cheese, grated

8 oz sharp cheddar cheese, grated *(reserve ¼ for the top)*

½ tsp salt

1 tsp baking powder

1 stick butter, melted

2 cans diced green chilies, drained

Toppings:

Salsa

Black olives

Sour cream

- Preheat oven to 350°F.
- Beat eggs and flour together in a large bowl; stir in remaining ingredients.
- Pour into a 9" x 13" greased casserole dish and bake for 35 minutes.
- Cut into 4" squares and serve with desired toppings.

Serves 8-10

Basic Omelet

3 eggs

2 tbsp butter

1 tbsp milk

Salt and pepper

Filling options:

Cheeses – American, Swiss, Muenster

Vegetables –sliced mushrooms, chopped tomatoes, cooked spinach *(squeezed dry)*, chopped onions, chopped green pepper

Meat- crumbled bacon, chopped ham

- Beat eggs and milk in a medium bowl.
- Melt butter over medium heat in an 8" fry pan.
- Sauté raw vegetables in butter then pour in eggs.
- When the bottom of the egg mixture is slightly firm, add desired fillings.
- Fold omelet in half and cook for about 1 minute.
- Carefully flip omelet and cook about 1 minute more.
- Sprinkle with salt and pepper.

Serves 2

Tomato Basil Tart

1 frozen 9" deep dish pie crust

2 cups Mozzarella cheese, shredded

5 Roma tomatoes, sliced and drained on paper towels

½ cup loosely packed fresh basil leaves, chopped

4 cloves fresh garlic, chopped

3 thin slices of onion, separated

½ cup mayonnaise

¼ cup Parmesan cheese, grated

- Bake empty pie crust according to package directions.
- Remove from oven and reduce heat to 350°F.
- Sprinkle the bottom of the pie crust with ½ cup of the Mozzarella cheese.
- Cool.
- Arrange tomatoes on top of the cheese and sprinkle the basil and garlic on top of the tomatoes.
- Top with sliced onions.
- Mix remaining Mozzarella, mayonnaise, and Parmesan and press over the onion slices.
- Bake for 1 hour.*

Serves 6-8

*FYI: Cover the edges of pie crust with foil to avoid burning.

Old Standby Sausage and Egg Casserole

12 eggs, beaten

1 can cream of mushroom soup

1 lb hot sausage, cooked, crumbled, and drained*

2 cups sharp cheddar cheese, shredded

- Preheat oven to 350°F.
- Beat eggs in a large bowl.
- Add remaining ingredients, mixing well.
- Pour into a greased 9" x 13" casserole dish and cook for 40 minutes or until casserole is puffy and lightly browned.

Serves 8-10

*FYI: Sausage may be cooked in advance for easier morning preparation.

Quiche Lorraine

One 9" unbaked pie crust

1 cup Gruyere or Swiss cheese, shredded

1 tbsp flour

2 tbsp onion slivers *(sautéed in 1 tbsp of butter until translucent)*

6 slices of bacon, cooked and crumbled

3 eggs

1¼ cups heavy whipping cream

¼ tsp nutmeg

¼ tsp salt

1/8 tsp pepper

- Preheat oven to 375°F.
- Prick bottom of pie crust with fork and place on baking sheet.
- Combine cheese and flour and place in the bottom of crust; then add the onions and bacon.
- Whisk together eggs, cream, nutmeg, salt and pepper; then pour over the top of the cheese, flour, onions, and bacon.
- Bake for 40 minutes or until center seems to be fluffy and set.

Serves 6

FYI: "Cream" is the same as whipping cream, often found in ½ pint cartons in the dairy section of the grocery store.

Scrambled Eggs and Salmon

2 tbsp butter

2 eggs, beaten

1 tbsp onion, chopped

½ cup salmon, cooked

Feta cheese *(optional)*

Toast *(optional)*

• Sauté onions in butter in a small skillet over medium heat.

• Add eggs and stir gently.

• Add salmon when eggs are almost cooked.

Good alone or on toast topped with feta.

Serves 2

Sausage Rolls

1 lb hot sausage

One 8 oz pkg of cream cheese, softened

2 pkgs of refrigerated crescent rolls

1 egg, well beaten with 1 tbsp of water *(egg wash)*

¼ tsp each of dill weed, cayenne pepper, and basil blended together

- Preheat oven to 350°F.
- Brown and crumble sausage. Drain.
- Mix the cream cheese with the warm sausage in a medium mixing bowl.
- Roll out one pkg of crescent rolls. Pinch the perforated edges together to form a solid rectangle.
- Spread ½ of the sausage mixture onto the rectangle, leaving a ½ border of dough on all 4 sides.
- Lightly roll up the dough, starting with the longer side and then place seam side down on an ungreased cookie sheet.
- Repeat with remaining sausage mixture and second pkg of rolls.
- Lightly coat the dough with the egg wash mixture for a golden, shiny, and brown appearance. Sprinkle with herb/spice mixture.
- Bake until golden brown.
- Carefully slice into rounds.

Serves 8-10

Easy Egg Muffins

2 eggs

2 slices Canadian bacon

2 English muffins, sliced, toasted, and buttered

2 slices cheese of choice (cheddar, Monterrey Jack, Swiss)

- Break eggs into 2 lightly greased coffee cups.
- Pierce the yolks several times and cover cup with a paper towel.
- Microwave on high for 30 seconds.
- Lay a piece of Canadian bacon on the bottom of the English muffin.
- Spoon egg on top of the bacon and cover with a slice of cheese.
- Microwave again until the cheese just melts (approx. 30 sec).
- Top with the other half of the muffin and enjoy!

Serves 2

Breakfast Burritos

2 eggs   1 whole wheat tortilla

1 tbsp butter   Grated cheese, salsa, sour cream

- Break the eggs into a small bowl and mix with a fork.
- In a small skillet, melt the butter over medium-high heat.
- Add eggs and stir gently.
- Roll the cooked eggs in the tortilla with desired toppings.

Serves 1

Stuffed French Toast

One 8 oz pkg cream cheese, softened

½ cup peach or other preserves

1 loaf Hot and Crusty Pepperidge Farm French Bread™, sliced

5 eggs

1¼ cups milk

½ tsp vanilla

¼ tsp cinnamon

Cooking spray

Optional toppings

Maple syrup

Confectioner's sugar

Butter

Fresh peaches or other fresh fruit

Whipped cream

- Mix together the cream cheese and preserves.
- Cut a 3" slit in the top crust of each slice of French bread and spoon approximately 1 tbsp of the cream cheese preserve mixture into each slit.
- Mix the eggs, milk, vanilla, and cinnamon together in a medium bowl.
- Heat a lightly greased skillet to medium high heat.
- Dip the French bread in the egg mixture, wiping the excess egg off on the side of the bowl.
- Place the bread on the skillet and cook on each side until golden brown.

Serves 6-8

Garlic Cheese Grits
A Sunday brunch standard

1 cup grits

4 cups water

1 stick butter

8 oz pkg Velvetta Cheese™, cubed

1 tsp garlic salt

1 egg

Milk

- Preheat oven to 350°F.
- Butter a 2 quart baking dish.
- Boil the water in a medium pan; stir in grits and reduce heat to low.
- Cook for 5-8 minutes, stirring occasionally.
- Remove from heat; stir in butter and chunks of cheese until melted.
- Slightly beat egg in a 1 cup measuring cup and fill with milk.
- Stir into grits mixture. Add garlic salt.
- Pour grits into baking dish and bake for 1 hour.

Serves 8

Granola-Yogurt Parfait

½ cup granola

½ cup plain or flavored yogurt

½ cup fresh fruit *(sliced or diced blueberries, strawberries, raspberries or peaches)*

- Place granola in a martini or other small shallow glass.
- Add yogurt and top with fresh fruit.

Serves 1

Seasonal Fresh Fruit and Honey-Lemon Dressing

4 cups assorted fresh fruits, sliced or cubed

Dressing

¼ cup honey

1 tbsp lemon juice

- Mix the ingredients together and drizzle over the fruit just before serving.

Serves 4

INDEX

Equivalent Measurements

Liquid Measurements

1 gal = 4 qt = 8 pt = 16 cups = 128 fl oz

½ gal = 2 qt = 4 pt = 8 cups = 64 fl oz

¼ gal = 1 qt = 2 pt = 4 cups = 32 fl oz

½ qt = 1 pt = 2 cups = 16 fl oz

¼ qt = ½ pt = 1 cup = 8 fl oz

Dry Measures

1 cup = 16 Tbsp = 48 tsp = 250 ml

¾ cup = 12 Tbsp = 36 tsp = 175 ml

⅔ cup = 10 2/3 Tbsp = 32 tsp = 150 ml

½ cup = 8 Tbsp = 24 tsp = 125 ml

⅓ cup = 5 1/3 Tbsp = 16 tsp = 75 ml

¼ cup = 4 Tbsp = 12 tsp = 50 ml

⅛ cup = 2 Tbsp = 6 tsp = 30 ml

1 Tbsp = 3 tsp = 15 ml

Dash or pinch or speck = less than 1/8 tsp

Quickies

1 fl oz = 30 ml

1 oz = 28.35 g

1 lb = 16 oz (454 g)

1 kg = 2.2 lb

1 quart = 2 pints

Substitutions

Out of something and in a hurry? try these:

Recipe Calls for	Use
1 cup self-rising flour	1 cup all-purpose flour *plus* 1 ½ tsp baking powder *plus* ½ tsp salt
1 T cornstarch *(for thickening)*	1 T all-purpose flour
1 clove garlic	1/8 tsp garlic powder
1 cup bread crumbs	1 cup cracker crumbs
1 tsp baking powder	1 tsp baking soda *plus* ¼ tsp cream of tartar
1 T fresh herbs	1 tsp dried herbs
1 cup yogurt	1 cup sour cream
1 cup white wine	1 cup chicken broth
1 cup buttermilk	1 cup whole milk *plus* 1 T vinegar

This Cookbook is a perfect gift for Holidays, Weddings, Graduations & Birthdays.

To order extra copies as gifts for your friends, please visit us online at www.lifeafterramencookbook.com

* * * * * * * * *

Cookbook Publishers, Inc. has published millions of personalized cookbooks for every kind of organization from every state in the union. We are pleased to have the privilege of publishing this fine cookbook.

883-09